Inside Ireland's Tax System

Dermot Byrne

Inside Ireland's Tax System.
by Dermot Byrne
Copyright ©2021 Dermot Byrne
ALL RIGHTS RESERVED
ISBN: 978-1-914488-06-1
Including the right of reproduction in whole
or in part in any form.
This edition printed and bound in the Republic of Ireland by

lettertec

Lettertec Publishing
Springhill House,
Carrigtwohill
Co. Cork
Republic of Ireland
www.selfpublishbooks.ie

No part of this publication may be reproduced
or transmitted by any device, without the prior written
permission of the copyright holder.

This book may not be circulated without a cover or in
any cover other than the existing cover.

*This book is dedicated to
the late Dr. Frank Brennan,
a friend and colleague
for many years.*

Contents

Introduction 1

Chapter One– Training School, Dublin 3

Chapter 2 – Thurles 13

Chapter 3 – Wexford 21

Chapter 4 – Enniscorthy 31

Chapter 5– Tansley Witt & Co 35

Chapter 6 – Frank Brennan 47

Chapter 7 – Media Career 53

Chapter 8 – Irish Tax Institute 57

Chapter 9 – Self-Employment 67

Chapter 10 – Conclusion 83

Introduction

In my final year in a Business Studies Degree course in Trinity College Dublin in 1972/73 I applied for the job of a tax inspector with the Revenue Commissioners. Most students were applying to accountancy firms to train as an accountant. The job did not appeal to me and the salary for the first three years was a pittance.

There were three careers available in the public service: administrative officer in the civil service, third secretary in the Department of Foreign Affairs and tax inspector with the Revenue Commissioners. A college friend who had joined the civil service, Declan Reddy, advised me that the tax inspector position was easier to get than the other two and it was the only one that gave you valuable skills sought by the business sector.

I duly applied and the interview went well as I had a good knowledge of current affairs and also had worked abroad in several countries. The interview panel asked me if I had applied for the other two jobs and I said no, which seemed to impress them and they were in a position to verify my answer.

After graduation in June 1973 I went to Denmark to work and used it as a base for travel in Europe. Just before Christmas of that year I had to return to Ireland for a civil service oral Irish examination.

My mother, a primary school teacher, was fluent in Irish and gave me some tuition and it came back to me fairly quickly. Rather oddly, I thought, the oral Irish examiner asked me in Irish if I felt that an oral Irish test was out of date in view of the Troubles then raging in the North. I agreed with him and pointed out that Garrett Fitzgerald[1] had mentioned this in a recent speech and that the public service had to embrace the two traditions[2] on the Island.

I did not receive any further communication from the Civil Service Commission for a few months.

---

1 Minister for Foreign Affairs 1973-77
2 The Gaelic Ireland Tradition and the Unionist British tradition

Vale of Clara, Co. Wicklow in Winter 1996.

Chapter One
– Training School, Dublin

In late March 1974 I was visiting friends in Co Armagh, staying in a house in Craigavon near Portadown. I called my home in Co. Wicklow to tell them where I was. My mother said to me that the Irish Revenue were looking for me to work for them as an Inspector of Taxes.

On 8th April 1974 I reported to Revenue Headquarters, Dublin Castle, signed the Official Secrets Act and completed a form to get a PPS Number. They sent me then to an office called Burton Chambers which was over a drapery of that name in Dame Street.

I was very well received there and met a large number of top officials. I did not realise then that they were the "Top Men" – they were all men in those days until later on. From there I was sent to Hamman Buildings in O'Connell Street where the Inspector of Taxes Training School was located. Again the manager, Sean Kearns, made me very welcome.

He explained the nature of the work which was essentially the examination of accounts and tax returns of tax payers or non-payers with a view to establishing the correct income tax liability. There were about 12 people altogether there and they were a mixture of graduates and people who had joined the public service from school and had by virtue of promotion been sent to the Revenue training school.

I was given two brief volumes of notes on the 'nature of a trade' and the 'allowable items of expenditure in determining the profits for tax purposes'. I noted that they were internally produced documents with a heavy emphasis on British case law i.e. decisions of the British courts. On reflection this was not a surprise as the Irish tax system was formerly the British system and post-1922 much of the tax policies in Britain continued to be adapted by Ireland.

The atmosphere was quite informal and I soon realised that being able to relate an amusing story or incident would help me get by. The county you came from was important with those of Kerry and Cork being the most predominant. GAA games were a big issue with them and they made fun of Wicklow football at my expense. This did not last long as I said I had played rugby[3] and had never actually seen a Wicklow GAA match. They looked at me with surprise but that vanished when another recruit from Cork, Kieran O'Connell, said that he was a sailor.

When work finished a few of my new colleagues invited me for a drink in the local pub on Cathedral Street, off O'Connell Street, known as "The Goalpost". In the spirit of the occasion we invited the manager Sean Kearns also and he was a most convivial companion. It was clear that he had good technical knowledge of tax but his people skills shone in the pub. In an interesting insight into cross-border co-operation he told us that in his youth he had played soccer for the Irish Revenue against the Northern Irish Revenue and there was an annual match on St. Patrick's Day. I got a laugh when I suggested that he should have gone as a GAA team to play them in the late 1950s.

The atmosphere was very friendly and the conversation and drink flowed until closing time. As recruits we heard stories which generally related to people and procedures in the job with the Revenue which appeared to us to stretch back to 1922. I felt under pressure to make some contribution and related that Hamman Buildings was called "the Block" in the Civil

---

3   My Granduncle, on my mother's side, Willie Fallon, was President of the IRFU in 1949-50. He had played with Bective but was more a "Blazer" or a team official than a player. He used to travel to Paris with the Irish team in the 1930s and always vanished on the Saturday morning to meet his friend Jim Joyce. It was only after Joyce died that the other Blazers realised that Jim was really James Joyce, the writer. They had been at school together in Belvedere and Joyce refers to "a boy named Fallon" in the final chapter of "Portrait of the Artist as a Young Man".

War and Cathal Brugha was shot as he came running out the front door with a gun in each hand. The group had not heard it before and were amused at the idea of a gunfight at the tax office where they worked.

After a few weeks looking at Revenue notes and the fundamental concepts of taxation we were given real sets of accounts to critically examine. The accounts were sent up from an office downstairs called Construction Industry District which dealt with building subcontractors in the Greater Dublin area. As this area included Co. Wicklow I knew some of the persons whose accounts we were asked to examine.

We all soon learned that a profit per the accounts was not a profit for tax purposes when dealing with sole traders. Firstly, the deduction for depreciation had to be added back and secondly the private use elements[4] – motor and phone expenses – had also to be added back. This revised profit for tax purposes was then subject to a claim for wear & tear in lieu of depreciation. The annual allowance for the latter was set by Accounting Standards while for the former it was set by law in the annual Budget. The rate of wear & tear can vary from 10% per annum to 100% per annum depending on Government policy and the nature of the expenditure.

The manager of the training school had previously worked as a District Manager in the West of Ireland. He told us that to properly examine a set of accounts you needed to see the records behind them. Under the then tax law there were only tax audits in circumstances where a desk audit had revealed serious errors or the taxpayer was subject to investigation for other reasons.

I understood very well why the manager had this view as my father, who was a timber merchant, bought his groceries in a shop that also sold

---

[4] Private use means the non-business use. As an example, a shopkeeper might use his car mainly for business use such as going to the cash & carry for deliveries to customers. However, he might go to a football match or to church at the weekend and that would be private use. A proportion of the annual running costs and wear & tear is disallowed as a business expense to reflect private usage of the car. This attempts to level the playing field for the car owner who has no business activity.

petrol and oil. He paid the shop monthly by writing a cheque the stub of which read "Petrol and Oil" while the shopkeeper gave him an invoice which only had the words "Petrol and Oil" and the amount due.

My father always felt that the Revenue were, as he said, "decent people". About 1960 he and a friend of his with a business in Glendalough went in to meet the tax inspector for Co. Wicklow whose offices at that time were in O'Connell Street, Dublin. His friend Jack had no records and the Revenue had an estimated assessment. The tax inspector tried to estimate the sales and the expense based on known dealings with a Government department. Jack could not agree with any estimate the tax inspector made and my father came away from the meeting with the opinion that Jack was an unreasonable man while the tax inspector was fair and reasonable.

One Friday Sean Kearns told us "you are all off to PAYE Units on Monday for practical experience of the operation of PAYE".[5]

I found myself in Unit 63 which dealt with the staff of the retail and distribution trade in the Dublin area. This was an attractive assignment for the recruits as the Revenue employees were generally girls of our own age. They used abbreviations in their speech. Staff was made up of CAs – Clerical Assistants, TOs – Tax Officers and HTOs – Higher Tax Officers. They were producing P21s – Assessments from Form 12s – Tax Returns. The unit dealt with oil tanker drivers and I was astonished at the level of their earnings.

The manager of the unit was an elderly woman who had worked for Revenue since leaving school. She did not welcome me to the unit and seemed to see me as a burden on top of an already full workload. At lunchtime the staff vanished. I tended to remain and read the paper and

---

5   PAYE is a system where income tax is deducted by the employer from a person's wages and the employer pays it directly to Revenue. It was introduced in the UK in 1944 and Ireland borrowed the UK model in full when PAYE began here in 1960. Documents such as a P60 and a P45 have found their way into everyday speech. The system was replaced with a real-time internet-based operation on 1st January 2019.

eat a sandwich. I quickly discovered that a lot of telephone calls from the public came at lunchtime as it was their only opportunity during a busy day to make a call. For a trainee the calls were difficult and the most I could manage was to take details in writing for the staff to deal with after lunch.

Given the volume of calls I suggested to the manager that she stagger the lunch break but she did not like it. She correctly said that "your role here is to learn rather than offer advice". I subsequently related the incident to Sean Kearns who was not surprised by the manager's reaction. He said that Unit 63 was under-resourced. He had a number of sayings garnished from years of working in a bureaucracy. One was "no man is hero to his successor" meaning that if you replace somebody you will often find his work was in arrears. Another saying was "never shit on your own doorstep" meaning if you were working as a tax inspector don't harass your neighbours.

One of my trainee colleagues, Philip Murtagh, was in a unit dealing with security firm staff. I realised Ireland is a small country when he rang me to say he had come across a letter from me saying that I had emigrated. In the previous year I had worked on a casual basis for a Dublin security company and was paid cash. The company had some sort of Revenue enquiry and the director told me to give him a letter that I had gone abroad. I duly did so and it turned up on Philip Murtagh's desk. We had a good laugh about it. I put Philip down as one of the most able people in the training school. He had fluent Irish, had a very high-class degree in science and was always dressed very well. To me he was a model tax inspector. He came from Co. Tyrone and played GAA. On the 12th July 1974 I went to Kylemore Bakery in O'Connell Street and bought an orange cake for tea break. Philip refused to eat any of it.

My sojourn in Unit 63 ended on 17th May 1974, much to the relief of the unit manager. At 5.15 p.m. I said goodbye to Breda Turner, the HTO who was teaching me the PAYE system. Fifteen minutes later she was dead having been killed by a car bomb in Talbot Street in what became known as the Dublin and Monaghan Bombings which claimed 34 lives.

Myself and Tadgh O'Connell, who was later to rise high in the Revenue hierarchy, were walking through Merrion Square Park on the way to a meeting of the Tax Inspectors Association in Earlsfort Terrace when we heard explosions. I guessed immediately that it was a car bomb and looked at my watch. When it was followed at two minute intervals by two more I was astonished.

When we got to the hall for the meeting in Earlsfort Terrace we were told that it was cancelled as the Garda Superintendent for the area wanted all buildings cleared. We found ourselves back on the streets which is the most dangerous place to be in a car bomb attack. There was evidence of real panic on the streets in Dublin city centre and the national phone system collapsed so that people in Dublin with relations in the country, as was typical in the Revenue, could not call home to say they were alright.

All that night and the next day rumours were rife that the city might be attacked again. It did not happen and within two days the media, based on informed sources, began to speculate that the culprits were from the Portadown area.[6] To this day nobody was ever caught and the crime is unsolved.

At the end of July I was sent to work in Dublin 9 Tax District which dealt with self-employed persons in the city centre. The office was in Lord Edward Street and the District Manager was Eddie Murray. We were told that he was hardworking and very well connected with the top people. Dress and punctuality were important. While working there the junior staff told me that the Knights of Columbanus were strong in Revenue. I never saw any evidence of this but currently the Wikipedia entry on the

---

6   For a detailed account of the events of that day see "The Dublin and Monaghan Bombings and the Murder Triangle" by Joe Tiernan 2004

Knights states that "at one stage they had a significant presence in the Revenue"[7].

The only slight run-in that I had with Eddie Murray was due to the habit of the inspectors going for a few pints at Friday lunchtime. On the last Friday that I was there Eddie smelt drink off me when we met in the corridor. He was a Pioneer[8]. He went to the most senior of the inspectors who were in the Pub – Tony Hanrahan – who was in fact the second-in-charge. Eddie said to Tony "Did you go out drinking with Mr Byrne at lunchtime". Tony being a natural diplomat said "I had lunch with Mr Byrne". Tony only had orange juice in the pub.

To restore the situation I dashed out to a nearby bookshop and bought "The Complete Poetry of Paddy Kavanagh" which I felt Eddie Murray would appreciate as he was from Monaghan and near to Inishkeen where Kavanagh wrote about. The shop gave me a bookmarker free with the book which I put into the book at the poem "House Party to celebrate the destruction of the Roman Catholic Church in Ireland". At 5.15p.m. I presented Eddie with the book and he expressed gratitude for my thoughtfulness. On Monday morning I related the incident to Sean Kearns in the Revenue training school.

To be fair to Eddie Murray he had already advised Sean Kearns that I had a good knowledge of business and the work in Dublin 9 District was no trouble to me. Sean said he was sending me to Dublin 11 District in St. Martin's House, Waterloo Road. It dealt with all professional people such as doctors, lawyers, and architects in the Dublin area. They were more likely to be high earners and have access to sophisticated tax advisers to reduce their tax exposure.

My tutor in St. Martin's House was Sean Moriarty who later became a senior figure in Revenue. The work was challenging but interesting

---

7 Wikipedia accessed on 1 July 2019
8 Member of the Pioneer Total Abstinence Association

compared to that of Dublin 9 District. There was only one visitor for the couple of weeks that I worked there. An accountant called in by appointment because his 1973 profits were a multiple of what he had declared for the two prior years. At the time my salary was about £2,100 per annum but the caller had declared a profit of about £30,000 for 1973.

I just listened in on the interview as it was a small office. It turned out that the accountant had several projects underway and they all came to fruition in the one year. Sean was happy with the explanation and the accountant left clearly relieved.

When he was gone I discussed with Sean Moriarty what I had overheard. He said he might be entitled to increase work-in-progress in prior years and thus increase the profits of those years. However, it would have reduced the profits of the year 1973 which were nearly all chargeable at the then top rate of income tax. It followed that the overall yield might be less with a lot of extra work. I thus realised that the job required not only technical knowledge but a good bit of common sense.

My only funny incident when I was working in St. Martin's House was that I sought a tenant to share the house I lived in at the time in Killiney. It was owned by my mother and she expected me to pay the overheads, which was reasonable. I advertised in the Evening Press. As the house was new and at that time it took two years to get a phone, I used the office number and my extension in St. Martin's House.

The first call I got was the source of some confusion for both the caller and myself. At that time the Revenue had an office in Pearse Street that perused the two evening papers, the Evening Herald and the Evening Press, trying to establish who the landlords were that advertised property to let who it assumed might not be declaring it on their tax returns. When the Pearse Street Revenue investigator rang the number given on the paper the switchboard said it was Revenue. This created confusion on a large scale. When the switchboard put the Revenue person on to me

I told him the cost and location and that I was a Revenue employee. He then laughed out loud and told me why he was calling. I quickly dropped the advertisement on the advice of the Pearse Street caller who said that one cannot use Revenue facilities for private gain. As a good sport he binned my adverts from his own records.

I returned to the Revenue training school in early September and we were all told that we were to be sent in the next month to work permanently in a country district. Sean Kearns arranged for a senior inspector with wide country experience to talk to us. This inspector was John Burke, then in charge of Dublin Farming District which dealt with all farmers in Dublin and the counties around it.

The substance of the talk was how to conduct oneself as an inspector in an Irish town. The occasion was too good to miss and I was the culprit with a practical joke. At the back of the room where Mr Burke had to speak I pinned to the wall Miss September 1974 centrefold from Playboy magazine.

As a professional to the core Mr Burke did not bat an eyelid. He delivered a description of a middling sized Irish town where the business and professional classes would look critically at the Tax Inspector. It was necessary to be impartial while at the same time being on friendly terms with everyone as one had to get on with people. He said that Head Office would be more appreciative of a person who managed to pluck the goose with the least hissing than somebody who annoyed the locals and got their backs up.

As all of us, plus Sean Kearns, sat with our backs to the centrefold on the wall. Sean did not notice it until Mr Burke had left. It was a tribute to Sean's people skills that there were no repercussions. My colleagues to a man said they did not know who put up the picture and maybe it was builders who were working across the corridor!

At the end of October we were all sent to work permanently in country Tax Districts and I was sent to Thurles. We reflected among ourselves on the six months of training. Everybody agreed that it was a useful life skill even if one switched jobs to something else. To quote Mark Twain, death and taxes are always with us. Colleagues had various gripes e.g. not being sent to their choice location, bored with the work etc. I said my only gripe was the old stories at social events and the conversation was not very interesting.

I had, at college, been forced to study public administration and avidly read Chubb's book The Government and Politics of Ireland[9]. In it he said that from his dealings with civil servants they did not tend to speculate broadly on matters and that the conversations tended to be mundane. I asked myself was Chubb[10] referring to the stories and recollections going back to 1922 that we had now heard many times. When I put that to my colleagues most of them readily agreed but maintained that it was part of the culture of the civil service.

---

9   Chubb, Basil: The Government and Politics of Ireland (1970) Oxford University Press
10   Basil Chubb was one of my lecturers in Political Science for a year in Trinity College (1969/70). In class I disagreed with him that the British civil service was better than Ireland's. I mentioned the Cambridge Five as traitors. (The Cambridge Five, then known as the Cambridge Three, were recruited by Soviet Intelligence while students at Cambridge University. They had high profile careers in the British civil service.) Chubb said they were the exception. He had a twitch in his neck every so often and one day somebody asked him how he got it. He said he was in the RAF during the War and was shot down over Germany. On the way to Stalag Luft III prison in Poland he was beaten by the SS Guards. This led to an awkward silence. To keep matters going I asked him what were the conditions like in the Stalag. He said it was quite good as the Germans considered airmen to be gentlemen. The 1963 film "The Great Escape" which starred Steve McQueen was based on events there. We always looked at Chubb with admiration from that day on. He was a true gentleman.

Chapter 2
– Thurles

I arrived in Thurles in late October 1974 and stayed for a week in the historic Hayes Hotel. On 1st November I had a few pints in the bar and got chatting with the Bar staff. With my interest in history I reminded them that the GAA was founded in the hotel exactly 90 years ago that day. On 1st November 1884 Michael Cusack chaired a meeting that set it up. The staff, being local, knew all about it. I enquired where the meeting had been held. One man said it was supposed to have been held in the bar itself but that officially it was not. Another said why not, since Guinness sponsor the GAA?

After a week in the hotel, I moved down the street to Dwans, the undertakers, who had kept tax inspectors for many years. Maybe, like Mark Twain, they linked death and taxes. They had a funny picture of a wake in the front hall with the caption "Where there is a will there are relatives".

In Thurles everybody knew everybody else and the majority of the Tax Office staff were local to the area. Hence, the local knowledge was very good but if there was an issue then the District Outdoor Officer, a Revenue grade, was a retired Garda who had the ear of all the stations in Tipperary.

My first job there was to complete cards which were ultimately for the Department of Finance. I had to check the profits for the most recent year available for the main taxpayers in the District and put the figures on the cards. The Department then collated all the cards from all the Districts to estimate the likely national tax yield for the Annual Budget.

As I was from a rural background the District Inspector gave me some farmers to deal with. The Finance Act 1974 had put all farmers with a rateable valuation of over £100 into the income tax system for the first time. The District had already issued an initial batch of letters and my brief was to follow up those who had not replied.

I sent out about 30 letters reminding people of the first letter and seeking a reply. To my surprise, within a few days, I had my first caller at the counter. I went down to the public office to a tough looking man who seemed somewhat indignant. He said that he did not think the taxman would find him in Newport for years as he was in the middle of nowhere and kept a very low profile. "How did yous find me"? I said the County Council had given us the names and addresses of all landowners in the district with a rateable value over £100 and his name was on the list.

Another early duty in Thurles was to attend the Circuit Court on behalf of Revenue. At that time estimated assessments were raised which were appealed to the Appeal Commissioners. If confirmed there was a further appeal to the Circuit Court. Myself and two other inspectors, Mick Mullins and John Quigley, went into the Judge's private chambers with the District Inspector.

Judge Sean MacDiarmaid Fawsitt snapped that his court would not be turned into a training academy for tax inspectors. Mr McGovern had to make a compromise with each of us coming into the judge's chambers when our allocation of cases was called. At the hearing I had an allocation of small pubs with no accounts for years and the judge was clearly not impressed that these matters should be before him at all. He told me to train myself to settle these cases without bothering him!

An amusing incident occurred around Christmas 1974 in Thurles. There was a sign in the public office "Má tá Gaeilge agat labhair í". Word went around the office that there was a need for an Irish speaker in the public office as there was an Irish speaking taxpayer seeking to discuss his assessment. Eventually a volunteer was found and apparently acquitted herself very well. The sign came down shortly afterwards.

I used to swim in Thurles pool which was very underutilised when I was there. Often there was a tall man that I discussed current affairs and history with after our swim. I knew him as a priest and it was quite a surprise when I learned that he was Tom Morris the Archbishop of Cashel and Emily – a very informal and well-read man. I had played squash in college and my colleague Michael Mullins discovered that there was a squash court in Nenagh which was quite a drive away. However, as each of us had a car we went there one night a week taking it in turn to do the driving. Michael's car had an immobiliser. He had bought it from a Ford worker in Cork and it was fitted with a device that cut off the petrol supply so that it could not be started. The switch to turn it on was hidden in the glove compartment. One morning Michael discovered that his Ford Escort was stolen. He reckoned that it was not that far away. We walked for less than 5 minutes and saw it at the swimming pool. The people that took it must have been exhausted after pushing it on the flat for about a quarter of a mile. Michael just got in, turned on the petrol switch and away he went.

Sone weekends I remained in Thurles as you got a better feel for the place if there at the weekend. Maire was Dwan's housekeeper and she used to sometimes check that I had been at Mass by asking me at lunchtime on Sunday "Who said Mass today?" I used to answer as best I could but one Sunday I said to Marie that I was not at Mass as I had an exemption from my swimming pool colleague Tom Morris. Quick as a flash she said "You need to have that exemption with you when you meet the Man above".

Dancing in Thurles on a Sunday night was at the Premier Hall. It was an old-fashioned affair like "The Ballroom of Romance" with the women on one side of the hall and the men on the other. I preferred the Disco at Clanwilliam Rugby Club near Tipperary Town. They were a very horsey set down there and a common pickup line was "Do you ride out"? With no horse and working in the tax office I was at a double disadvantage.

The biggest social and business occasion in Thurles was the Munster Hurling Final. On the Saturday before the game various musicians and hawkers of all sorts would arrive in Liberty Square. On matchday thousands of fans would arrive and they were anxious to spend money. Pubs, restaurants and hotels did a roaring trade. Everybody was well behaved and there was little evidence of vandalism or hooliganism after the game. The gatemen at Semple Stadium were standing their friends a pint for a week afterwards. By repute the official attendance was as wide of the mark as the official figure for the number of people really unemployed in the county. The former was underestimated while the latter was overestimated.

The tax inspectors used to drink in Maher's pub at the top of Liberty Square. The publican was a very decent fellow and also had a very good sporting pedigree. If you were too long in the pub his wife would arrive out with sandwiches for which there was no charge. In my first week in Thurles we watched live from Africa at 3a.m. Irish time the famous Ali v Foreman fight known as "The Rumble in the Jungle" in the pub. When it was over, at about 3.45a.m. Mrs Maher served us tea and sandwiches. You never got that kind of service in Dublin!

In most pubs in Thurles the tax inspectors were not really welcome. It was felt that we might be assessing the trade and on duty when in the pub. There were stories, part of the Revenue culture referred to earlier, that a previous District Inspector used to stand outside shops and count the number of customers entering the shop over one hour. If true, it was not official policy and very likely a stupid way to conduct oneself in a town where everybody knows everyone else.

A local accountant that I was dealing with on a number of cases invited me out to lunch one day. He said that relations between the profession and the local Revenue were not good. It appeared that a previous District Inspector had written to various accountants enquiring about their qualifications and it was not the same inspector that was reputed to stand outside the shops to count the customers. I said if it was a commercial outfit it seemed that they would appoint a PR person right away to improve their public image.

Thurles was at that time one of the smallest Tax Districts in the State. It did not have Nenagh as that was dealt with in Limerick while in the south of the county the Clonmel area was dealt with by Waterford Tax District. Apart from the local Irish Sugar factory there was little industrial employment. Tourism seemed to be non-existent and no tourists were visible on the streets in the summertime. The State seemed to be the largest employer, particularly the education sector.

At a follow-up lunch, where I paid, I debated with my accountant friend that there was a two tier system in operation. As a public servant I paid my tax every fortnight under PAYE but the self-employed were paying it often years in arrears. In my allocation of work at least half of the assessments were under appeal for several years. As no returns or accounts were submitted the collection system was stuck. He said that he knew what I meant but from the other side of the fence. Half of his clients were un-cooperative but that VAT had brought about a small change as he now had interaction with them every two months instead of once a year.

We both agreed that Revenue should offer an incentive to recalcitrant taxpayers to get their affairs in order and up to date. He said that it would mean more business for him with less hassle if there was a stick and carrot approach. At his suggestion I drafted a short paper on the subject and sent it to Revenue HQ in Dublin. Two weeks later I had a call from a very senior official who thanked me for my thoughts. However, as I was in reality suggesting a tax amnesty at the expense of co-operative tax payers it was a matter for the Dáil and not Revenue.

With the passing of the Finance Act 1974 the farmers with a rateable valuation over £100 came into the income tax net for the first time. Thurles was quite dependent on the agri-sector apart from the sugar factory. It was clear from the tax office records that agri-contractors, farm machinery suppliers, livestock hauliers etc were underrepresented in them and it was going to change due to the farmers now being taxable. In effect the change brought in a large subsector that appeared to have escaped income tax up to then.

I got to know an agri-contractor socially and he was always looking for VAT advice which he described as a curse as none of his farmer clients were VAT registered. One day I asked him why all his queries were on VAT and none on PAYE. He said that he had a few off duty Gardaí as part-time workers which was seasonal and he only paid them cash. I suggested one full-time man would be safer as he could claim a tax deduction for wages. My friend said no as that man would be no use to him if he was caught with no road tax on his jeep or exceeding the speed limit and they arrived already trained in agri-work as they were all farmers' sons. Such was the rural economy at that time.

The pub trade was still an attractive sector in 1975 in the country. People who returned from England or the USA with money or who got a large settlement due to an accident would buy a pub. Very often they knew next to nothing about managing a pub which was very demanding with a 7 day week operation and very unsocial hours. Many quit and sold out after a short time as there was always a good demand for pubs.

In my allocation of work there were a large number of rural pubs with large arrears of accounts and tax Returns. I felt that some of them were making money and laughing at us. One day while reading the local paper I got an idea. There was a page or two of notices where publicans were applying to the local District Court to renew their licences. A local solicitor told me that the purpose of the advert allowed the local Garda Superintendent to object to the renewal of the publican's licence but that was a rarity in Co. Tipperary. Armed with this information I suggested to a senior colleague now deceased, that we go to the District Court and object to the renewal of the licence for those publicans who were in arrears with their tax returns. He looked at me in amazement and said that if we did that we would be run out of the town. A decade later Revenue solved the problem by requiring a Tax Clearance Certificate in order for a publican to renew the pub licence.

In my final weeks in Thurles we had a Tax Appeals Hearing. It was largely an exercise in procrastination. An accountant would appear with a list of his appeal cases. The Appeal Commissioner (AC) would say to the accountant acting for the taxpayer, is the Tax Inspector's estimated income assessment accurate? The accountant would answer that it was not but he would need another four weeks to provide the accounts. The system required the accountant to furnish accounts for the business to displace the Inspector's estimate. The final income tax liability for the year was based on the accounts. If no accounts were provided, the Inspector's assessment was accepted and the appeal was dismissed. A limited number of adjournments could be allowed in order for the accountant to complete the accounts but at some point, the AC would say final adjournment. Thus, if it appeared before the AC again it would be confirmed.

There were always some bad cases that would be confirmed. The AC was an experienced accountant or lawyer and he would ask questions of both the accountant and the inspector as to evidence of profitability. He might then, either confirm the inspector's figure or fix a lower figure which he felt was more reasonable. Unlike today there was a further right to appeal to the Circuit Court.

At the end of the AC Hearing come the "No Agent cases" i.e. where the taxpayers represent themselves. One of them was memorable. He was a haulier with a substantial estimated assessment on him. His body language was aggressive. The AC asked him what he had to say about the estimate on him. The haulier said "I would not tell a fellow from Dublin anything". The AC politely explained that he was being un-cooperative and he, the AC, had power to fix the assessment . The haulier calmed down a bit and said "Anyway, I have not got any money to give you." AC - "What has happened to your money?" Haulier "I have a wife and 4 young children to keep and I just built a new house." AC "What did it cost?" Haulier "About £15,000 sir." AC "Have you a mortgage on it?" Haulier "No sir, I paid the builder as it was being built."

The AC turned to me and said "Mr Inspector, what do you say?". I replied that the taxpayer had built a new house out of his cashflow and the estimated income may be in fact too low.

Without bothering to look at me or the taxpayer the AC wrote in his book and said "assessment confirmed".

For me and I guess for the haulier it was a classic lesson in how not to run a business. Do not go to a Tax Appeal unless you know the ropes. Without offending the taxpayer the experienced AC had got a picture of the true size of the profits by a few seemingly innocent questions. As he was leaving I told the haulier to go to an accountant, my friend, and do so today as he could appeal to the Circuit Court and file accounts. You have to treat the public fairly and the man seemed very industrious.

About a week later the District Inspector was transferred to Dublin and was replaced by John Hussey. I was sent to Wexford which the Revenue staff regarded as a plum posting.

Chapter 3
– Wexford

I arrived in Wexford on 27th July 1975 in the middle of the tourist season and was lucky to get short-term accommodation in White's Hotel, literally next door to the Tax Office which was located in the Ulster Bank building. The PAYE section was located in Anne Street where all of the Tax Office is now based.

The contrast between Thurles and Wexford was remarkable with more sunshine and less rain and generally much more evidence of prosperity. By Irish standards the town was cosmopolitan compared to Thurles.

The District Inspector, Sean O'Brien, was very friendly and gave me a mixed allocation of work consisting of most types of taxpayers that reside in the county. He acknowledged that, as in Tipperary, there were substantial arrears in that the returns were outstanding and many were un-cooperative. However, he said that he considered the quality of the agents i.e. accountants who submit the returns was quite high by the standards of the time.

The staff told me that Sean O'Brien was easy to deal with and tended to be very informal. That he went to school in Cork with Jack Lynch but was the kind of man who would never use that connection for his personal advancement.

My office had very large north-facing windows and in the distance I could see Curracloe Beach and the forest behind it. The immediate view was of the harbour and what some of the locals called the "New Bridge" built in 1959! Altogether a very pleasant setting.

My appointment to Wexford filled a vacancy which was there for a while. There was some unworked post linked to my allocation. Much of the post was first-time farmer accounts for 1974/75 being their first time in the income tax net. When I examined a sample of them I discovered a very high opening stock figure and a low closing stock figure and an overall loss. As all had a land rateable valuation of over £100 the farm operations were large and the losses were large as well.

I discussed these accounts with Sean O'Brien and he said to get stock figures and values and compare them with CSO statistics and see if they were accurate. He said that HQ wanted to get the farming sector in its entirety into the income tax net without much controversy. In other words, he felt I should agree the figures that were reasonable. I started to read the Farmers Journal to get a feel for the trading position but pessimism was widespread.

A colleague told me that, in a seminar for would-be journalists in Dublin, they ran a competition for the most unlikely headline. The winner was just two words "Happy Farmers". I decided that the large farms were typically breakeven or small profits rather than making large losses. It proved to be an uphill struggle to show that the losses were bookkeeping losses rather than real losses. I was satisfied that farming was not giving an adequate return on capital employed. The wives of these farmers tended to be teachers or nurses with off farm employments.

The husband's farm loss could now be offset against their salary to recover all the PAYE suffered in 1974/75. If farming had not come in the income tax net it would not be possible to get a refund.

Some of the other business activities in the allocation were more complex. One large hotel had computations of capital allowances that took up a full A4 sized page. There were also some foreign-owned companies which had the benefit of the export sales relief rules meaning that the profits attributable to export sales were tax free. By local Wexford standards they were large employers – that was the reason the tax holiday was given and it clearly was working well.

I had to vacate White's Hotel after two weeks with nowhere to go. There was a sort of bed in the Tax Office canteen so I moved there until I sorted out accommodation. The paper keeper, Dinnie O'Brien, used to be the first in each morning and he would make me tea. He said his wife would make me a breakfast and he would bring it in. I declined his marvellous generosity. Another inspector said not to forget to declare the benefit-in-kind from Revenue on my tax return! At last I got accommodation near the Theatre Royal in a very old part of the town.

In early September I got a memo from HQ to say that I had to do an examination in taxation at the end of that month in an office leased by Revenue from the ITGWU (Irish Transport and General Workers Union) in Liberty Hall. The main part of the exam involved quoting verbatim sections of the Income Tax Act 1967. I had no interest in such an exercise and just summarised the sections in the exam.

Needless to add the Revenue was not happy with that and sent me a memo to say that I was not successful and that a Tom Kirby would call to see me about my efforts. He duly called to the Tax Office one day and said that he was the senior examiner. The meeting did not go well as he said they wanted the Act quoted verbatim on the basis that the test was one of endurance and obedience rather than an intellectual exercise. He felt that if one knew the Act by heart then one's work would be more productive.

My opinion, which he visibly did not like, was that it was a pre-1922 British method of training which was inappropriate now and he merely took down the Crown and put it in his pocket and put up the Harp.[11] He said that this was the way things were done and he had 50 years in

---

11   For a discussion on these matters see Chapter 2 of History of The Revenue Commissioners by Sean Reamonn (1981) Institute of Public Administration

the Revenue and one could not improve on the language of the Act. I countered that if that was correct then the Courts would be unnecessary. We parted on the basis that I would repeat the exam and make a better effort to meet his requirements.

Tom Kirby then went to see Sean O'Brien who was my boss. Sean told me afterwards that he had asked Sean what was my attitude to work. Sean assured him that I was a good worker and had an exceptional knowledge of business practise. Sean confided to me that he personally did not get on with Tom Kirby and gave him no change. He said Tom left with a puzzled expression on his face and remarked that Revenue would be better off without these college fellows!

My colleagues in Wexford were Mel O Cuinnegáin and Seamus Mooney. I used to play squash with Mel once a week in the Farmers Kitchen Hotel on the Rosslare Road. He was a very good soccer player and still plays the game (2019). His father will be well known to students of 20th Century Irish history as the founder of Ailtirí na hAiséirghe who were prominent in the 1930s and 1940s. Seamus Mooney was a cross country runner and a member of a local athletic club. I once ran six miles with him and found it hard to walk for a week afterwards. Later Seamus was Citizen of the Year in Wexford – not bad starting with the handicap of being a tax inspector! My then girlfriend and now my wife, Mary O'Neill, was a voluntary worker with Wexford Opera Festival. A fellow volunteer of advanced years took her to one side one night to tell her that if she continued to be girlfriend to a tax inspector she would have no friends.

With the paper keeper being Dinnie O'Brien and the Inspector in Charge being Sean O'Brien this led to confusion. This was all the more marked as Dinnie wore a pin striped suit while Sean had a raincoat. Dinnie was at the lower grade but sartorially the roles were reversed. Dinnie had, in the early 1960s, worked on the construction of the Government Offices in Anne Street and got a job there when the Revenue moved in. He told me that when he walked past another building site in the town occupied by his former colleagues they would look at him in the pin striped suit and sing "All because the Lady loved Milk Tray" from the TV advert. Jealousy got them nowhere.

After a few months in Wexford I got my bearings and as a sort of hobby would check to see if shops within sight of the Tax Office were in the tax system. To my surprise I discovered some were not. I raised the issue with the District Inspector and he said you must treat the public evenly. I did not know who was in the tax system in New Ross as I had not checked up there but I could not discriminate against the people who were our neighbours. I readily agreed with him. If I ever needed local assistance Eric Wallace was the Outdoor Officer and his judgement always tended to be sound and impartial.

Sometimes when working for Revenue one gets an idea that a certain sector is more profitable than they let on. I decided it was the fish and chip shops but I had little success with queries on their accounts. One day I saw under special notices on a national newspaper that one of my "clients" was making an application for Irish citizenship. The notice said that if one knew any reason why he should not get it then write to the Secretary, Department of Justice in Dublin. I showed the notice to the District Inspector and the fact that the man was not co-operative with the Irish tax system and asked him should we write to the Department of Justice to oppose his application. I was told no and that the enforcement methods available to Revenue would eventually collect the taxes that he might owe.

Taking the long view, one could not make a lot of money in an Irish town without it coming to Revenue attention. This might be by way of a property purchase, motor cars, racehorses, holidays etc. In the country money does not shout – it roars!

Computers were starting to make an appearance and instructions were sent by post to Dublin Computer Centre. The most common one in my allocation was 'Stop 16' which stopped collection. It could often be due to the amount being estimated and excessive. As my family were in business I was well aware of the volumes of paper being generated in the name of Sean Patrick Bedford, then the Collector General, that had deluged the country. Generally they were estimates and nobody took them very seriously. This in turn had undermined the collection arm of the State.

I often found myself in sympathy with the tax agents where they had made an error in the returns. The entries had to be a mismatch with some figures being from the prior year and some from the current year. No attempt appeared to have been made to streamline it. The calculation of child allowance appeared to be of extreme complexity for no obvious reason.

Worst of all was the appeals system. The inspector raised an estimated assessment on the taxpayer based on known information on the file e.g. the profits in previous accounts or the acceptance of an estimated assessment in the past or very often non co-operation. An appeal would then arrive but no payment.

Eventually the Appeal Commissioner would attend at Wexford Courthouse to hear the appeals against the assessments. With an allocation of 300 businesses, I had about 150 appeals but no returns or accounts submitted. The idea of the listing of the appeals before the Appeal Commissioners was to force the taxpayer to submit returns or in their absence the estimated assessment might be confirmed and the tax then became due.

At my first Wexford hearing on a Monday morning the Appeal Commissioner, Mr McDowell,[12] began the hearing by asking the five inspectors present what they thought of the international rugby match

---

12   Father of Michael McDowell who was Attorney General 1999-2002, Minister for Justice, Equality and Law Reform 2002-2007, and Tánaiste 2006-2007

on the previous Saturday. As the others were GAA men I gave him my opinion of the game and he offered me his. As a result I could not put a foot wrong when my cases were called.

Generally in my allocation as in indeed in the others the problem was that the accountants who were the tax agents could not get the records out of their clients in order to prepare the accounts. The accountant would request a postponement of a month and generally the Inspector would say no objection. However, if this was the 2nd or 3rd listing then the Appeal Commissioner could refuse or say final adjournment. Where he refused any further adjournment he would turn to the inspector and enquire if the assessment was reasonable? The inspector would then give the results of the last accounts or state that there were no accounts for years. The Appeal Commissioner would then use his own experience to fix the assessment for that year and thus release the tax for collection.

While this looked like a farce to me it was only half the story. The taxpayer's agent, the accountant could then appeal the confirmed assessment to the Circuit Court and the whole process would start all over again. Typically it would be another year before the assessment was before the Circuit Court. In the interim most accountants would have got the accounts done and submitted with returns to the local Tax Office.

Believe it or not the farce continued until 1987 when the World Bank looked at the volume of income tax held up in appeals and demanded that the 19th century British system be replaced by self-assessment which had become widespread in other countries. The following year the self-assessment system with penalties for late filing and field tax audits were enacted.

One can reasonably ask why did we not see the light before the World Bank saw it. In large organisations there is a tendency to do things the same way for years without question. If new ideas did not work then the inventor gets the blame. If they do then the people at the top took the credit. At least that is what I heard in meetings held at the time. Careers are at stake when there is a personal file on everyone kept by a superior. It's the East German Stasi on a small scale and I could see that it clearly inhibited initiative and also decision making.

As in Thurles, the top earners in Wexford District tended to be doctors, solicitors, large company directors and chemists. There was a sprinkling of old moneyed very wealthy people with investment income and extensive property interests. The vast majority of the population were on small incomes. I dealt with one man who had a shoe repair business and he declared a profit better than most of the shops in Wexford town. On further checking I discovered that he was Jehovah Witness and they take their tax obligations very seriously.

I had a slight disagreement with Sean O'Brien on the assessment of priests. He told me that I was accepting their figures without question and he doubted in some cases if they were true. My view was that I if I wanted to make money I wouldn't become a priest. Sean's retort was that if I wanted to make money I shouldn't become a tax inspector either. I did challenge a few accounts but they proved to be correct.

Generally the early filers of tax returns were members of the Church of Ireland with the Roman Catholic brethren a poor second. I never got a rational explanation for this although one senior inspector told me that the Church of Ireland people get their reward in this life and the others expect it in the next!

Pubs at that time were still considered profitable businesses and in many places it was the only business apart from the shop/post office. Revenue tried to establish the profits in a pub by taking the difference between the sales price and the cost price of the 10 most popular lines of drinks. This gave them what was called in accountancy parlance the 'gross profit'. Revenue then deducted the overheads as declared in the accounts to get the true taxable profits.

A publican in Galway produced a booklet called "100 Ways why I can't get the Revenue Gross Profit". Typically this might be the local football team won the County Final and he had to stand a free round for the entire bar or the barman stole the takings for years and it would only be discovered when the barman suffered a serious illness and was out of work. Other less common reasons was severe competition, shebeen pubs in private houses, customers afraid to come in as the Gardaí were sitting outside at closing time etc.

The Revenue view in all this was that the publican had his hand in the till plus wages were paid out to unregistered staff saving VAT on sales, income tax on profits and PAYE on wages.

I was at many appeals and Revenue was never guaranteed success and often there was a compromise. For anyone who had tried to run a business it is never as simple as it appears. In my view a pub can be a very complex business with one day off a year now that Good Friday closing has gone.

Sean O'Brien had spent many years in Wexford Tax District and knew most of the businesses quite well. He told me not to accept claims for a write off of bad debts without getting a proper explanation as he said there was a rural practise of settling for 50% but in cash. A few weeks later I brought to his attention a claim for a write off in a large shop and asked him should I pass it. He picked out two people from the list called S...... and told me to check if they were not solvent as people of that surname tended to be well off! In both instances his suspicions were well founded. I had to advise the accountant that the bad debts write off would have to be critically reviewed by the accountant without disclosing what I knew.

The summer of 1976 was the best for many years and my girlfriend Mary and I were on the beach at Curracloe every evening for nearly three months. Learning sections of the Income Tax Act off by heart was not something I spent any time doing. Unfortunately I had to go to Liberty Hall to do the Revenue exam again. Tom Kirby said "Mr Byrne, you are late". I replied "I am not significantly late". He gave a slight smile as he knew the words appeared in part of the tax legislation. The others doing the exam overheard the exchange and were more than surprised as they were afraid of Tom Kirby. I had forgotten the episode but a Dublin tax advisor, Gerry Higgins, who was there, reminded me of it at the Irish Tax Institute Annual Conference in Galway in 2018 – 42 years later.

The result of the second exam was no different as I had not got the sections off by heart. Sean O'Brien was anxious that I stay in Revenue and he told me he had given me a good report for my "Stasi" file unlike his predecessor. At that stage I had my allocation up to date and asked Sean could I work in VAT for a few weeks to widen my experience. This he arranged and I went about as assistant to May McDonnell who was the VAT Inspector. The experience gained over a few weeks stood to me for many years in a variety of occupations. Getting income tax wrong and one might owe a few thousand but get the VAT wrong and one might owe a hundred thousand!

Sean O'Brien District Inspector asked HQ if they had any other jobs as I had no interest in their exams. To my great surprise they said they had what was called a non-technical inspector. They acted in a wide variety of roles but did not have to do the exams that the technical inspectors did so it seemed ideal for me. The non-technical inspectors were, to my mind, very able people and I felt the distinction between the two grades was more academic than real.

I was considering my options when out of the blue James Sheil, who had the largest accountancy practise in Wexford, phoned me to say he had a job for me. When I called to see him in Enniscorthy he showed me 12 letters from me on farmers' accounts that were not yet answered. I soon found myself working there and replying to Revenue correspondence with Your Ref: DB and Our Ref: DB. Needless to add I said that the writer of the letter did not really understand the position. In the circumstances where I was the author of both letters nobody could contradict that.

Chapter 4
– Enniscorthy

In Enniscorthy I swapped my view of Curracloe for that of Vinegar Hill but was still close to the beaches of Co. Wexford. The local people would tell you about 1798 as if it had happened a few years earlier. The oral history tradition is very strong in the town. There was also a rebellion there in 1916 which was very unusual given that actions outside of Dublin were very limited.

The accountancy practice had a large cross section of business and professional clients with many very long established companies. The farmer-owned co-ops were the biggest clients and absorbed a lot of time. Due to a change in the law many of them were in the tax net for the first time. There were also plans for mergers and the issues could be very complex.

We sometimes had to attend public meetings of farmers on co-op proposals. There would be no shortage of opinions and speakers from the floor. I put it down to the fact that they were working on their own all the week and were delighted to find an audience on which they could vent their frustrations.

My primary function in the firm Sheil Kinnear was to review the draft accounts produced by the audit department for tax planning issues. I realised very quickly that it was in fact more important to look at the allocation of expenditures that made up the basic accounting entries in order to save tax. When one had dealt with that issue then the subsequent tax planning issues were of lesser importance and would just fall into line once you knew the tax rules and the latest developments.

The audit staff prepared draft tax computations and generally they were pretty good with one or two exceptions. One that I always recall was a provision for the close company surcharge on the deposit interest of a co-op which had about 1,000 members. Readers of this book who are tax practitioners will know that a close company surcharge only arises where a company is controlled by five or less people, so the surcharge obviously does not apply to a co-op of 1,000 members.

While Sheil Kinnear dealt with many tax districts my old district in Wexford was the principal one. My ex-colleagues were happy to deal with me as a single contact point in the firm and we settled a large number of disputes by compromise. James Sheil said that some of them went back years and he was very surprised at the settlements.

I was invited to Revenue social events and James Sheil encouraged me to get involved as he said confrontation was of no value to an accountancy practice. Often he said win or lose an appeal argument case it was hard to get paid. He bemoaned the fact that the accountants did not control the funds like solicitors do in litigation cases.

In April 1978 I attended my first Irish Tax Institute seminar in Waterford on the Finance Act 1978 and given by Frank Brennan. As we had not met since 1974 in Dublin we recalled the days working in Dublin 9 and 10 Tax Districts. Frank said that there was an opening for a tax consultancy firm in Dublin to provide advice to accountants and solicitors. I said that I saw opportunities for tax planning in farming using the notional system but would anybody pay for it? We agreed to keep in touch.

I was very impressed with the way Sheil Kinnear was organised and how they processed the work once they got it in. James Sheil said that he had about 25% of clients who were uncooperative and he had even made attempts to get rid of some of them without much success. He believed that the practice actually lost money on these clients as it took so long to produce a set of accounts from what were incomplete records. He added that he had no objection if I tried a heavy-handed approach based on my Revenue experience.

Armed with the list of hard cases I phoned them to say that the Tax Office in Wexford had been in contact and they were considering the client for prosecution and their names would be in the Wexford People or the Echo newspapers. It had an immediate effect on about 60% of the persons that I had contacted, particularly those who were involved in GAA clubs, parish councils etc. They felt that if their names appeared in the paper they would have to quit their position. We received the records for most of the larger uncooperative clients in this manner. However, there was still a hard-core number who refused to cooperate and yet refused to go away. Half in jest I said to James Sheil that in college I had come across a management theory book which said that if you have a number of nuisance clients in a professional practice the solution is to make a staff member, whom you do not like, redundant under terms where he takes on the nuisance clients. The book said that people would jump at this opportunity. James was not a humorous man but he laughed at this theory for a long time and agreed to look at it.

The secondary function that I had in Sheil Kinnear was to manage the personal tax returns and maintain a quality control on it. As I was new to the allocation it was quite demanding as lacking personal knowledge of clients you are a severe disadvantage. Again the audit staff prepared draft returns and their quality was good but I had to read over each file to get a handle on the client.

A large number of them were conservative farmers who were now in the tax system for a few years and kept good records. I was very surprised with the size of the funds they often had on deposit in the local bank.

They tended to be industrious and thrifty with very modest expenditure on themselves. Often one of their chief concerns was of succession as their children were going to college and nobody was that keen on the farming life or so they told me.

I now found myself attending the Appeals Commissioners from the other side of the fence. The usual candidates who were non cooperative were on the appeals List. I did not make much effort to defend them and admitted the true position to a Mr Egan, Appeal Commissioner at the time. He took me at my word and confirmed the estimated assessments. While I had to appeal to the Circuit Court, the result of the appeal hearing did force them to produce records sooner rather than later.

Sometime about mid 1978 through my work in Enniscorthy I came into contact with an old Dublin accountancy firm called Tansley Witt. They had a lot of clients in Co. Wexford and the managing partner, David Fleetwood, asked me to meet him in the Talbot Hotel when he was next in Wexford. He was sporting a Fáinne[13] when we met which was not something one saw very often.

He explained that they had a nationwide practice with international links and that their tax person had left after only a year and they needed an urgent replacement. While the money was good I felt uncomfortable about leaving Enniscorthy after less than a year. I went to James Sheil and told him that I had a quandary and that I would not leave if he matched the Dublin offer. He said he knew Tansley Witt as they had large clients in Wexford and he could not match their salary levels without upsetting all the other senior staff in the office. To be fair to him he offered a compromise based on increments over five years but I declined and found myself in Dublin in August 1978.

---

13   Pin badge worn to show that the wearer is able to and is willing to speak Irish

Chapter 5
– Tansley Witt & Co

The Tansley Witt office was at 10 Fitzwilliam Square[14] in a beautiful Georgian terrace of houses looking out on the square. The square was not then open to the public but each resident or business in the square had a key.

The Tansley Witt practice had been set up pre-1922 and a lot of clients were involved in importing and distribution. When the State was created the senior Irish-based staff of British-based manufacturers quit their jobs and set up in business as Irish-based agents for the manufacturers. These companies were very resilient and survived the high import tariffs of the 1932 De Valera Government, the Economic War with Britain and the Second World War shortages. In the 1970s a period of consolidation set in and many of them were gobbled up by large firms. This did not affect the auditors as long as their client was doing the acquisitions.

The practice had clients literally all over the country and even in Northern Ireland. One of my first assignments was to go to Derry to provide tax advice to a firm of accountants there who were not that familiar with the Republic's tax laws. All went well the day I was there and at lunchtime I was shown Duke Street where the famous confrontation with the RUC occurred on October 5th 1968 which has been shown many times on

---

14   As a child I attended parties in No. 9 Fitzwilliam Square. My mother's first cousin, Eileen McGrane, used to live next door and the old hands in Tansley Witt recalled her. She was a friend of Michael Collins and her flat at 21 Dawson Street was one of his offices in Dublin in the 1920 to 1922 period. She was a student in UCD at the time and later got a Master's Degree at the Sorbonne Paris. She is mentioned in several recent books. See Page 3 of "Michael Collins – The Man and the Revolution" by Anne Dolan and William Murphy (2018) Gill Books.

television. However, I got an unpleasant surprise in the evening when I left the practice to go to my car. The staff came out of a shirt factory nearby and confronted a British Army patrol of mainly black soldiers on the street where I was parked. "Get back up in the trees" were among the mildest expressions I heard. When I got back to civilisation I said danger money and not travel expenses would be needed next time. The next week they sent me to see a client in Kinsale, altogether more pleasant surroundings.

Because of the large scale operations of their clients, tax planning issues were of far greater importance than in my previous employments. Case law and precedent became important and I purchased all the publications on Irish and UK case law and compared the clients' issues with the authorities. As Tansley Witt tended to refer complex legal issues to a tax counsel I took to offering my view in advance of his. Fortunately for me we seldom differed. A large number of publications on Irish tax began to appear and the Irish Tax Institute was to the fore in organising lectures on new developments. This significantly reduced the pressure on tax advisors to furnish correct and timely tax advice.

The 10% Corporation Tax rate came in from 1980 for manufacturing clients. We had a large number of grey area cases in grain drying, bagging coal and light assembly where we did not know if the claims would succeed. In order to reduce uncertainty we met senior Revenue officials who were positive that a generous interpretation would be taken of the new 10% rate activities. Some cases were not clarified for years but we took a liberal view of the reliefs. Fortunately the High Court did also and generally our assumptions on the availability were ultimately found to be correct.

With the advent of the 10% rate the Export Sales Relief (ESR) holiday was phased out. However, if one had a company which had made exports before the end of 1980 it could continue to have the ESR holiday for a number of years. This presented me with a commercial opportunity. I incorporated a new company and bought some timber products with it which I exported to a garden centre in Co. Antrim. In early 1981 when no new ESR company could commence I advertised it for sale. Believe it or not I had a buyer in a few days. A prominent Dublin builders providers gave me £13,000 for it! What they bought was the ESR span of relief as the company had no other assets.

On the personal tax side, some of the clients were far wealthier than those I had dealt with in the country. In fact one family was reputed to be the wealthiest in Ireland and owned several large estates in Ireland and vast estates abroad. They lived in the grand style with a butler greeting you at the door. Tea was served by a valet. The family were very charitable, making extensive donations to various bodies. A problem arose once where Revenue obtained third party details suggesting that a family member's disclosed income was incorrect. When I sorted it out with Revenue in a very favourable manner for the family, they invited me to dinner with the family. I had my own valet for the evening!

One of the clients was a large construction group of companies. They had sold some Dublin sites to an Isle of Man company and the purchaser onward sold them to another company in the Isle of Man. Eventually another Irish group company purchased those sites at their current market value. The Revenue did not like this and every so often there would be an appeal hearing which would have to be adjourned on some technical ground. The Tax Inspector was a very pleasant and reasonable man called Joe Connellan and he used to apologise for the appeal listings. Similar issues were later resolved in favour of the taxpayer in the famous Supreme Court decision of 1988 known as *McGrath v McDermott (Inspector of Taxes)*[15]. The following year a general anti-avoidance provision was enacted in section 86 of the Finance Act 1989 to deal with artificial transactions.

---
15 [1988] I.R. 258

I was not long in Tansley Witt when I asked to sort out the UK and Irish tax affairs of several Lloyds underwriters. It was a very steep learning curve. The members of Lloyds were wealthy people who were in effect using their assets twice. Firstly the assets might be in a factory or farm or in shares on the stock market and secondly they were pledged against risk in syndicates managed by professional risk managers. At that time to be a Lloyds "name" as they were called one also had to have £100,000 surplus cash at the bank available at short notice to meet claims. As the "name" was trading in a personal capacity then liability was unlimited and one's entire assets were "on the line".

Notwithstanding the risk, I came across several people who wanted to join Lloyds. It carried social prestige with proof that one was wealthy and also admission to exclusive London clubs.

The tax work involved combining the results of all the syndicates which involved liaison with Lloyds and then the preparation and submission of returns to the UK Revenue. As these clients were Irish tax resident, the Lloyds income had also to be declared here and claims made for appropriate Double Tax Relief. Some accountants that I came across regarded the work as a nightmare and passed their Lloyds work to my firm. Once one had mastered the complexities then the work could be done fairly quickly and as it was a mystery to most people fees were never a problem.

In the mid-1980s serious problems arose at Lloyds and the people who had earlier been trying to get in were now trying to get out. It turned out, for reasons of bad luck or maybe design, that the London risk managers had put "Paddy" into syndicates covering American health products and medical insurance and huge claims would have to be met by the Irish based "names".

Some people's assets were wiped out overnight. It came as a terrible shock to many as they had become conditioned to good results. Efforts were made to transfer assets to spouses with one client who tried to do the reverse. He said he was acting in trust for his wife and she was really the "name". I enquired as to her assets and he said "very little apart from an account at Brown Thomas". I advised him to tough it out and perhaps it would not be a severe as predicted in the final runoff of the account. After the Lloyds crash we saw very little Lloyds work and the knowledge that I had acquired was quite redundant.

We had a large number of argument cases at the Appeal Commissioners and were successful in many of them. In the early 1980s Revenue began a PAYE blitz of pubs in the Dublin area. These were easy pickings as very often casual wages were clearly seen to exist in the final accounts of the pub. Revenue realised that the declared amount was not necessarily the total and onsite visits became common.

We had a client with a large pub in Leinster and Revenue discovered that the tips went to the owner who then administered them for the staff. Revenue sought VAT from the tips. We lost at the Appeal Commissioners but won at the Circuit Court. After the court hearing, I called in to tell the client the good news. To my surprise he seemed to take the win for granted which annoyed me as I hoped to get the firm a decent fee out of the win. The publican then said "Ah the Judge was in here last week – a very chatty fellow!"

In a West of Ireland case we claimed that a coal storage yard was a structure which merited Industrial Buildings Allowance. The mechanised handling of coal had already been given the status of manufacturing. Revenue said the yard was just the ground surface with a bit of cement. I used a quantity surveyor as an expert witness and his evidence won the case. It demonstrated for me the importance of the expert in an argument case.

We had one most unusual appeal. The late James Stafford, who was a prominent businessman, had an investment in an Irish satellite that was never launched. We said it was plant and claimed wear and tear on it against total income. Revenue said that since it never went into space that the trade had not started. For informed readers see Judge Rowlatt's decision in the *Birmingham Cattle By-products* case[16]. As Revenue hired an ex-Attorney General to represent them we engaged legendary tax counsel Tommy McCann to represent us. The Appeal Commissioner ruled in our favour.

The senior partner in Tansley Witt was Mr Bradbury and everybody called him Mr in conversation with him. He was of the old school and also wore a waistcoat and fob watch. He was the most knowledgeable man on tax relief for health expenses that I ever met. I used to put it down to the fact that he had a lot of elderly clients who had one foot in the grave.

He was very good at dealing with Revenue people and could sum them up well to his advantage. One day he sent me to Dublin Castle to get share transfer documents stamped. Let's say the parties were Jim Murphy and Hugh Murphy. When I presented it at the hatch the very stern woman said to me are these people related? I said that they were father and son. She said that it would have to go for adjudication. I made an excuse and took back the document. I returned it to Mr Bradbury with details of what the Revenue woman said.

A week later he showed me the Share Transfer Form stamped with some glee. I looked at it and it said Jim Murphy and Hugh Arthur and pointed this out to him. He said Arthur is his middle named and he then wrote the word Murphy after the word Arthur on the Transfer Form.

In my opinion the Revenue did not lose out here as the transfer values were for full market value. However, at that time if the issue went to adjudication one might not hear any more for up to 12 months. This gave the clients who were paying our fees some advantage.

---

16   *Birmingham and District Cattle By-Products Co Ltd v IRC* [1919] 12 TC 92, which is the leading case on when a trade commences.

In fact Mr Bradbury had the most beautiful copperplate handwriting that I have ever seen. It was so good that it was impossible to forge his signature as one colleague discovered when he tried to give an employee a good reference on the firm notepaper.

Mr Bradbury was very knowledgeable on Companies Registration Office (CRO) documentation which I knew nothing about prior to meeting him. Soon I thought I knew everything. The staff asked me could I form a limited company to act as an investment vehicle for their holding of shares quoted on the Stock Exchange. At that time the biggest company formation agent in Dublin was John E Nolan in Hatch Street. I used the format of one of his companies and sent it to the CRO. Six weeks later we had the certificate of incorporation.

Gerry Daly took it around to AIB to open a bank account. Several staff looked at it and he saw them take the Memorandum and Articles of Association into the manager's office. Ten minutes later the official came back to Gerry at the counter and said that this company has no borrowing powers – I had overlooked part of the Articles when copying them. The official said that AIB would open an account but would not lend the company any money. Gerry said that was fine as it was not intended to borrow to buy quoted shares. Somebody at the CRO tipped off John E Nolan about our plagiarism and a month later I had a letter from Mr Nolan to cease and desist and that he wanted damages. We ignored it.

The Managing Partner, David Fleetwood, was a prominent figure in accountancy circles. He had got first place in the accountancy exams and was Chairman of the Leinster Chartered Accountants for one year while I worked there. He could converse in Irish on any subject including Accountancy Standards and other technical issues. Like many prominent professional people in those days he was a member of a Gentleman's Club on St. Stephen's Green. One day in 1982 my assistant Annette McHugh and I accompanied David to the Club to meet a wealthy client for lunch.

As we waited in a small ante-room I noticed staff carrying a table and four chairs out of the dining room and setting them up in the corridor between there and the front hall. The head waiter then approached us and in a low voice whispered to David that they could not serve a woman in the dining room! We had a nice lunch but one had sight of the dining room which was half empty. This was 1982 not 1882.

David Fleetwood had a very earthy inner city Dublin client adept at practical jokes. One January day this client, let's call him Jacko, said to David "would you like my calendar? If I bring it in will you put it up? David said yes as he thought Jacko had his own business calendar which was a popular concept in the 1980s. Anyway a few days later Jacko arrived in with the Pirelli Calendar featuring ladies wearing a smile and not much else. Jacko said to David "you agreed to put it on the wall" so David attached it to the wall behind the desk at floor level so it could not be seen from the other side of his desk. We heard later that Mr Bradbury, who was a frequent attendee at Church of Ireland services, was less than amused when he noticed it.

In January 1982 there was a heavy snowfall in Dublin and Jacko came in to the office leaving his van parked outside the Italian Embassy next door. The double yellow lines outside the Embassy were covered in snow. Two Italians saw Jacko leave the van and go into our office and came running in after him. "You parked on double yellow lines" they exclaimed. "We are the Embassy". Jacko looked out the window at the snow and said " I see no double yellow lines". The senior Italian drew himself up to full height and shouted "You are Mick the mouse".

One of the daily features of life in a professional office with nationwide clients is to read the morning papers' death notices. What could be more embarrassing than to miss a client's funeral or that of the close relatives. A leading member of a Wexford business family died and David Fleetwood went down to Wexford for the funeral. David was a member of the Church of Ireland but in ecumenical 1980s he felt that he should partake of the Holy Communion. After the mass the widow of the deceased berated David for taking Holy Communion as he was a member of the Church of Ireland. It's very hard to please some people!

Tansley Witt changed their name to Binder Hamlyn which was an international network of firms. We used to go to somewhere in England each year for the Annual Conference. Some years it was spartan – student residence at York University. One year my wife decided to go with me, paying her own way. The venue was the Grand Hotel in Eastbourne, a very upmarket five star hotel. Mary paid £200 sterling for one night but could not afford meals which started at £50 sterling. She noticed a fish and chip shop in the High Street and went there. The proprietor, a rough looking fellow, said to her "I haven't seen you before, do you live around here". Mary said I am staying at the Grand Hotel. He said "I have been here since the War and you must be the first guest from the hotel to eat here!"

Tax schemes were in vogue in those days. Wealthy people liked tax schemes. It gave them a sort of one-upmanship over others. Clients came in to me with schemes that they read about in the papers or heard from the barman in the golf club.

Practitioners may recall the Reverse Nairn Williamson or the Capitalised Rental Schemes. My favourite at the time was the conversion of shares to debentures and if held for more than 21 years the rate of Capital Gains Tax then was nil. It was a legitimate cash extraction scheme.

Tax schemes can produce a lot of fees quickly for accountancy firms but often had a very long tail, meaning that years later they might create very trying Revenue correspondence. It was important to document everything and keep it available should it be required.

The heart of most of tax schemes were cash movements which were supported by minutes of meetings. One had to be careful not to fall into the trap of one Dublin company secretarial expert at a tax appeal hearing. Learned counsel noted about 20 meetings reflected in minutes all held on the same day. Counsel asked the expert in the witness box how long each meeting lasted. The expert said "This meeting 20 minutes, the next 30 minutes etc." Learned counsel added all the times up and it came to 22 hours. The case (and scheme) was thrown out by the Appeal Commissioner reportedly due to lack of reality.

In the mid-1980s the Government began to take steps to tighten up the tax system. At that time it was possible to get a state contract or an IDA grant yet have serious tax arrears. A system of Tax Clearance for State work was introduced so that the left hand and right hand could function together.

The new system soon produced results. A publican called to see me to say that he could not renew his seven day pub licence as he had arears of PAYE and VAT. The licence had expired three months ago and the local Garda Superintendent had called in to tell him to close down. I called a senior contact in the Collector General's office and secured an instalment arrangement. It was a struggle to get the 12 post-dated cheques out of the client. He was going to see his local TD to protest about the changes. The reality which I told him straight was that he was operating the business using the Collector General's money as working capital. He went to his bank to pay the taxes but was told they did not lend for tax liabilities. Eventually he got the Tax Clearance Certificate and renewed the Licence and did not fall into arrears again.

The Government also took tax collection out of the hands of the Civil Sheriffs and appointed Tax Sheriffs with specific instructions to deliver a speedy service. We had a client with a restaurant which had chronic tax arrears. The new Sheriff arrived and took away the furniture. The client was very resourceful. Next day he was open again as a take away establishment.

Personal tax returns could cause a lot of trouble in getting fees paid. With company directors the fees were frequently paid by their companies as part of the annual audit. If there were no company then the fees were very price sensitive. I recall some of the worst clients being retired people with little to do who queried everything that came from Revenue and the Collector General. In those days every 15 minutes of one's day had to be accounted for in the charging system. When the full costing was sent out to a difficult client he might call the partner to berate him. The partner might do a PR job as best he could. If that failed he could politely tell the client to maybe go to a small practitioner. Generally they did not go.

VAT returns also assumed a great importance as if one got the returns wrong due to using an incorrect VAT rate then the liabilities could be enormous. It became essential to do a VAT review as part of the annual audit. Also, if a VAT inspection were notified it became normal to conduct a pre-VAT inspection review. While prudent, it was also dangerous as if you missed what the Revenue later found then you could lose the client and face possible litigation.

Certain activities such as catering, tourism and farming were very seasonal and they had a lot of casual staff. Often they were on the dole for some or all of the week. Incredibly, even though paid by cheque, many got away with it for years. In the late 1980s, Revenue and the Department of Social Welfare got together using the latest computer systems and the unique PPS number that each person had to stamp out abuses. Social Welfare got copies of every employer Form P35 and with this simple exercise they could detect people "working and signing" as the official parlance went. Joint investigation units were set up by Revenue and Social Welfare and they made unannounced visits to business premises where they were already in possession of some evidence of irregularities. Prosecutions followed and Revenue set up a press office to supply local newspapers with details of court actions to deter others.

Sometime in 1988 Frank Brennan, whom I had known since 1974 when we both worked for Revenue, asked me to join his study group which met monthly. It was somewhat intimidating as most of the members were authors of books and were experts in some area of tax. I conveyed my views to Frank but he said not to worry as there were way too many single tax experts and far too few generalists in the group.

Binder Hamlyn merged with three small firms in 1988 and moved to expensive offices in Nassau Street in Dublin city centre. The working atmosphere turned poor with an apparent desire that staff work afterhours or at the weekend with a view to promotion. At least that was what I was told. Some of my old colleagues left but I decided to stick it out to see what would happen.

As a result of my involvement in Frank Brennan's group, he asked me to join him as he had a huge workload. I agreed but told him I expected to be sacked shortly where I was and would join him the next day. He thought this was very funny and said that he would do his best to have me sacked.

Things deteriorated in the tax department of Binder Hamlyn. There were about eight people working there – two died of rare illnesses and one was killed in a road accident – all young people. It was with some relief that I was sacked. One of the reasons given was that I was too harsh in correspondence with Revenue. My reply was that it was Revenue who trained me to write like that. I duly took Binder Hamlyn to the Employment Appeals Tribunal and the case was settled on the steps on payment to me of substantial compensation.

Chapter 6
– Frank Brennan

The day after I parted company with Binder Hamlyn, I started with Frank Brennan in Ranelagh. He gave me a stack of letters from 80 firms of accountants looking for tax advice. Some of the queries were fairly routine but a few were from the then new development of tax audits which were becoming common, while others related to complex schemes that Frank had earlier provided. In order to deal with these queries I had to understand the schemes. The work was demanding as one was dealing with very experienced accountants who often sought a new approach or a second opinion on a problem for what was their biggest client. One learned to provide balanced advice so as to give value for money but not to leave the firm open to litigation from the client for incorrect advice.

As Frank Brennan had a national reputation for tax competence the firm attracted a fair share of celebrities seeking tax advice. Frank told me to agree fees early with them and to get paid. He had found that they felt he should be honoured by their patronage and did not see why they should also pay him! I recall him winning a major case in the Circuit Court for a leading racehorse trainer only to be told after the win that the trainer had no money but would offer valuable tips in the future. At one stage Frank bought a racehorse and put it with a trainer client (not the one that could not pay the fees). About a year later we were at some racing function and I introduced Frank to a steward as a racehorse owner. Frank corrected me to say he was a horse owner as the racehorse turned out to be useless.

Frank Brennan & Dermot Byrne at Glenview Folk Park, Co. Leitrim on 2013 John McGahern Tour.

My new employer had a reputation for providing tax schemes. They had several on the go notwithstanding that the Finance Act 1989 had just brought in the first general anti-avoidance tax legislation. The intention was to put Ireland in the same position as the UK where the famous court case *Furness v Dawson*[17] had struck down artificial schemes. The UK has no written constitution so that court decision cases have greater impact there than in Ireland in tax planning. Frank had opinions from several barristers that the new legislation would be found to be unconstitutional. This did not turn out to be correct.

The most popular schemes then are what are now known as section 817 schemes. With that scheme a company which had substantial cash reserves subscribed for shares in a new company where the shareholders in the subscribing company controlled the voting shares of the new company. It used the funds it had got for the issue of shares to purchase a block of shares in the original cash rich company. If the person who owned the shares being sold to the new company was over 55 years of age and had been in business for 10 years he could get up to €750,000 out of the company tax free. A married couple could double this to €1.5m with no tax.

There were also several schemes which required an Irish person to move abroad to avoid Irish Capital Gains Tax. Favoured countries were Portugal, Italy and Malta at that time. In my experience, it is a rarity for a person to move abroad for tax purposes.

In the mid-1970s an earlier generation of high net worth business people went to Spain to avoid Irish wealth tax. I was aware that for many of them things did not work well due to alcohol, marriage breakups and business failures in Ireland due to their absence. My advice to people who talked about going abroad for tax reasons was to see if they would go for commercial reasons and if yes we can then work on the tax reasons and not the other way round.

---

17 *Furniss v Dawson* [1984] STC 153

Sometimes it can take years for a tax scheme to get an airing at an appeal hearing. The section 817 type scheme eventually came before Appeal Commissioner John O'Callaghan in Kerry in 2005 and he found in favour of the taxpayer. I acted for Frank Brennan at the hearing. Since then the legislation has been amended several times but in my experience it is considered to still not be watertight.

Moving to Portugal has been constrained by amendments to the Double Tax Treaty between Ireland and Portugal which did take quite a while to get through Portugal's parliament. However, new countries appear every so often and tax tourists are still with us.

The various tax schemes have also to be considered in the light of what is now called Section 811 general anti-avoidance provisions which was originally section 86 of the Finance Act 1989. There are very few cases reported where Revenue has used Section 811 and there seems to be a reluctance to use it. Instead they seem to rely on other specific legislation to defeat a tax scheme.

Frank Brennan was very sociable and would host a table at the Tax Institute Annual Dinner every year. Prominent people, clients and lawyers, would be at the table. I was delegated to sit beside Tommy McCann, the leading tax senior counsel, as he was at school in Ampleforth College in Yorkshire where my relation Eugene Byrne (Abbot Herbert) was in charge when Tommy was there.[18]

Working with Frank Brennan one could not avoid his wit. As proof he could entertain 700 people in the Burlington Hotel with a tax lecture which from anybody else would be dead boring. My favourite was the

---

18   Eugene Byrne was from Croney which is just a mile from the Vale of Clara, my home in Co. Wicklow. The family was prominent in English public life. One of them, Sir Laurence Byrne, was the High Court Judge in the famous obscenity trial of 1960 on D H Laurence's Book "Lady Chatterley's Lover". Abbot Herbert's sister May Byrne was a close friend and Godmother to my Aunt Mona, my father's sister. In 1962 when I had to decide on a boarding school May Byrne said that Abbot Herbert wanted me to go to Ampleforth at reduced fees as no Byrne from Ireland had ever gone there for 40 years. I kicked up a fuss and my parents relented and sent me in September 1963 to the nearest boarding school to my house which was Presentation College Bray.

cross-border pig smuggler. At one time there was a subsidy per head in Northern Ireland for pigs from the Republic of Ireland to help sustain the local bacon factories in the North. A lorry load of pigs were stopped at the Newry customs post, a vet was called as they seemed unwell. He examined them thoroughly and concluded that they had travel sickness. They had gone through the customs post three times already that day to collect the subsidies each time. The case was proved by CCTV which showed no delivery by that lorry to a bacon factory at all that day.

On another occasion Frank was driving to Kilkenny and got lost. Eventually he came to a crossroads when a sign said "Kilkenny 12" but in two separate directions. Eventually a countryman came walking along with a dog and Frank asked him which way he would go. The man thought for a while and then he said but I am not going to Kilkenny!

Like an artist Frank could invent a tax scheme but the aftersales service might not be ideal. One individual, subject to Revenue investigation, could not get any reply from Frank and arrived up from Galway at the Ranelagh office, refused all promises by reception Staff and sat outside Frank's door for two hours while he was at a meeting inside. Suddenly Frank, aware of the situation, came out and greeted the man warmly, gave him a signed copy of his latest book on the Buyback of Company Shares and was gone.

He was capable of a severe putdown but rarely used it. I recall being at a meeting of about 12 people, mostly lawyers, in a Big 6 legal practice and Frank was the only one there with no tie or suit. A solicitor in very posh tones was contradicting Frank's view of Trusts and catching sight of the solicitor's surname on a letter he said "where are you from"? The reply was Ballybackward Roscommon. Frank said I know Billy X there, to which the response was "he is my father". Frank said "Jaysus, he was the dirtiest footballer I ever played against. He tried to give me a kick in the balls when the ref was not looking! "Needless to add the room was in stitches and the poor solicitor was mortified, as they say in Dublin.

The Leitrim GAA team was doing well when I worked with Frank. They asked him to get them corporate sponsorship with all his high finance contacts. He would ring some prominent business person looking for sponsorship. The usual response was why should we give them money? Frank's reply was that they are going well at present and their captain is a member of the Church of Ireland. Sometimes he did secure donations but it was hard going.

Every year Frank organised tours of John McGahern country around Leitrim and Roscommon. As a bus load of 40 people travelled along the boreens Frank would give a running commentary on that townland and its people and how they appeared in McGahern's novels. The last tour was in the year of Frank's death in 2015 and the highlight was a visit to Arigna Mines which is now a museum. We had a wonderful few days with Irish dancing, visits to folklore centres and great food, drink and conversation. Frank had become an authority on McGahern and was often invited to literary events as a guest speaker.

He would sometimes tell a story against himself. One time he was at a reception in Strokestown Park House and he was there a bit too long. With nowhere to go the caretaker let him sleep in the main bedroom of the house which, while fully fitted out, had not been slept in for about 30 years. The next morning Frank, with a severe hangover, was awoken by a very worried caretaker to say that there were 20 ladies from the Sussex Georgian Society downstairs on a House tour and would be upstairs in five minutes. Frank had to make a hurried exit.

Despite having lots of business, Frank's practice was not well managed. He delegated that to others. Eventually he had to downsize due to cash flow problems. In 1992 he asked me to take over a block of accountants that he did not want and to start on my own but working in co-operation. I was to put his name on my notepaper and be available to assist if for any reason he was not available for work. His health had begun to deteriorate and people were starting to express concern at his appearance. He did take medical advice and his health improved.

His longstanding and loyal last employee, Pauline Atkinson, a company secretarial specialist, retired in 2008. Frank worked on his own from then onwards, his health continued to deteriorate and he died in the Mater Hospital on 1st September 2015. Cardinal Sean Brady gave the oration at his funeral.

Chapter 7
– Media Career

My first newspaper article on tax issues was about farming tax published in the Irish Times in 1979. While working in Enniscorthy for Sheil Kinnear & Co I had realised that the legislation was very loose and could easily be abused. After my article appeared the Revenue issued a circular to staff to advise them that the provisions of the Official Secrets Act 1963 also applied when staff had left Revenue employment.

The article was well received in newspaper circles and I got several offers to act as a regular contributor to national newspapers. The most attractive offer that I got was from Brian O'Connor, then business editor of the Irish Press group and I went with them. I had to produce a piece every two weeks or so under a pseudonym and it generated quite a few letters to the editor who was Tim Pat Coogan.

My endeavours were greatly assisted by a true blue Dubliner who worked for Revenue and made contact early on offering insights into Revenue thinking and proposals for legislation. At some stage the business editor expressed some concern about the contents of some articles in case their disclosure was a breach of the Official Secrets Act. However, I was able to assure him that no such breach had occurred or was contemplated.

Budget day was always a very pressurised day for me as I had to produce a budget summary for Tansley Witt & Co clients and get it to Sheriff Street post office by a certain time for distribution all over the country next morning. Then I had to dash to Burgh Quay and assist with the production of the Irish Press for next day. Commentary on the tax changes was no problem but the tables which had to be produced were a nightmare. One had to calculate the tax for the single person, the married person with one spouse working, the married person with both spouses working and the retired couple. The tables then had to apply a range of incomes to each category and then have it all furnished by 10p.m.

The 1982 Budget was memorable. I was leaving Burgh Quay about 10p.m. when I was called back by the porter. When I went upstairs everyone was crowded around a small black & white television and the RTE man was saying that Deputy Kemmy had voted against the Government because of VAT on children's shoes. As a result the Government fell. It had never occurred before in the history of the State.

We had to scrap what had been prepared and I wrote a general commentary on the history of budgets. Around 11 p.m. we got a budget summary from a large Dublin firm of accountants complete with a photograph of their Tax Partner requesting that we publish it the next day with their budget comments. To do so would have caused them severe embarrassment as they were obviously not listening to the radio and did not realise that the Budget had fallen.

Next day I heard another embarrassing story for a nationwide accountancy firm. The Dublin Head office had their budget summary done by 9p.m. and their partner set off for Portlaoise which was to be the rendezvous for the distribution of copies to the various provincial offices. He had his radio turned to a pop music station and did not hear that the Budget had fallen. However, those travelling to Portlaoise to meet him had RTE Radio on and they all turned back. When the Dublin partner arrived in Portlaoise there was nobody to meet him. He rang the Head Office but there was no answer as they had all gone home. In desperation he called the Managing Partner at home to be told that the Budget had failed. At that stage he must have been one of the few people in the country who was not aware of what had happened.

Various magazines were paying me for articles on tax matters. One day, Dan O'Hara, partner in Tansley Witt & Co told me that he had read a very good article on the new 10% tax rate on manufacturing and offered me a copy. When I looked at it in a magazine called the "The Irish Exporter" I realised that I was the author. When I told him he was a good bit surprised.

Norman Bale who was a famous tax advisor and author asked me to write an article for his Irish Tax Review on the taxation of forestry. This led to me being an occasional contributor to that publication which is the leading tax commentary in the country.

In 1989 the Sunday Business Post (SBP) began publication and their first editor Damien Kiberd asked me to produce as much material as I could as long as it was fresh and original. I quickly realised that the SBP was read by senior Revenue people and wealthy clients. The former often referred to my articles in subsequent phone calls or meetings as a result of my main work as a tax advisor. The latter read it avidly even though they might reside in a very remote location. Frank Brennan told me that the local newsagent in Co. Leitrim got three SBPs and 200 Sunday Worlds but the three SBP readers were worth more than the 200 Sunday World readers.

Around this time Revenue opened a press office with a view to using the media more effectively to convey their message. Decisions in Revenue's favour in the High Court began to appear in the national newspapers. Reports from local Courts on convictions for failure to lodge tax returns and such like started to appear in local newspapers. This is a very good method of fighting tax evasion.

Sometimes an article in the SBP might generate some controversy. Twice articles were mentioned in the Dáil by politicians and sometimes one would get irate calls from business people that I was flagging things to Revenue. This reassured me that I had an audience. My brief was to try and steer an independent path. Editors had no shortage of lobby group articles pretending to be educational or news. The editor of the SBP in 2006 showed me an article sent in by a large firm of auctioneers which indicated that if it was not published prominently they might pull their advertising. The gist of the article was that three bedroom semi-detached houses 20 miles from Dublin at €400K were good value!

Every trade has its own tricks. I was not long working for the Irish Press when a journalist working there was pointed out to me as "Disgusted Mother of Eight". Apparently he wrote letters to the Evening Press complaining about mannequins in Clery's shop windows in O'Connell Street which had very little clothes. The idea was to generate correspondence from real letter writers. I believe this tactic is still with us. If one listens carefully to some late night phone-in programmes on radio you will sometimes detect a caller with extreme views. This person is very likely an actor complete with fake Dublin accent.

I appeared on RTE Prime Time a few times to speak on tax issues. Last time I was on that programme I got a call the next day from an Irish client living in Spain to say that she saw me on RTE which she could access in Spain. Apparently in those days most Irish people who were permanently resident in Spain were able to watch RTE there. I also did several chat show programmes with Newstalk and always got on well with George Hook who was very professional with a good grasp of tax issues.

Since 2012 I have penned a monthly tax article for the Wicklow People/Bray People which is my local paper. It has been the source of several new clients including one man who was farming 1,000 acres in the south of the county but had no accountant.

One lesson that I have learned from extensive experience in journalism is that if there is an apparent error in an article, one will get calls. If its 100% correct you will get none.

Chapter 8
– Irish Tax Institute

As I had been a regular attendee at the Irish Tax Institute (ITI) events, I was invited to join one of their committees about 1998. I soon realised that one could get a lot of useful information for my work through involvement with the ITI. It was a classic voluntary work situation with the more work you put into it the more you got out.

Frank Brennan retired from the ITI Council and like in the Dáil he said that he was giving his seat to me. Anyway, the electorate did not agree and I missed it by seven votes. Fortunately there was a vacancy a few months later and I was co-opted to the Council as the highest vote getter not elected. Frank's advice to me was to keep two rules:

1. Not to be intoxicated at meetings between ITI and Revenue.

2. Not to be in the company of a lady, who was not my wife, at ITI social events.

I joined the Tax Administration Committee as I was a small practitioner and they needed more of them involved in the ITI work. This committee turned out to be a bonanza for me in terms of information and contacts. I also got involved in the Dublin Area Branch discussions with the Revenue which was most helpful for my work. However, sometimes I found myself doing work for ITI while my own work was neglected. One can't have it every way.

I quickly learned that the ITI Council was mainly a Big Four accounting firm operation in that nearly everybody was either a current employee or previously trained there or now worked for a Big Four client. I had previously suggested in an article in the Sunday Business Post that tax audits then, unlike now, were rare for Big Four clients and Revenue was too immersed in small business. Needless to add this was not well received at ITI and a Council member advised me that it would be useful to my ITI career to write articles praising the Big Four contribution to Irish business. I replied that there were plenty of such articles in the media and I was from the SME sector. I discussed the matter with a senior ITI staff member. This person pointed out that the recruitment of senior staff by ITI tended to be from the Big Four Firms to ensure similarity of culture between the Big Four and ITI. This was quite a surprise to me.

When I joined the ITI Council I gave the senior people an undertaking that its proceedings would never find their way into the newspapers. Some were concerned about this but they were quite satisfied with how I dealt with the matter. That issue never arose again.

As a Council Member of ITI one is expected to chair one of their committees. My job was Chair of the East Southeast Branch which was made up of 12 counties apart from Dublin. This structure was new and part of my brief was to create sub-branches in each county which broadly corresponded to Revenue Tax Districts.

Over a period of six months a sub-branch was created in each county using local practitioners as members. Staff of were good at finding suitable people. I did locate a few. Some practitioners were self-conscious, as being very small firms they did not feel justified or confident to be involved. Others were enthusiastic as they felt direct contact with Revenue would be useful for the profession and for their own practices.

It became the norm to meet Revenue once or twice a year and discuss issues and reflect on how matters might be improved. These meetings, in turn, fed into a Joint Revenue/ITI Annual Conference where the national picture was examined in a relatively informal setting.

The chairpersons of the various regional branches in turn reported to the ITI Tax Administration Committee which met quarterly to deal with problems associated with the national tax assessing and collection systems. These meetings were invaluable for my own work as what was a national problem would also be mine as a sole trader.

While I was offered the chairmanship of the Tax Administration Committee I had to decline it as with the Celtic Tiger roaring I was always under severe pressure to keep my own work up to date. My preference was to have a passive role and record relevant developments for my own practice. This was the opposite position to most of the other members of the Committee who were from large firms. They confided that if they were not promoted within the ITI it would look poor on their CVs within their own firm.

Often I made representations at the Committee on behalf of others who had lobbied me for some action in a specific are of tax policy. These representations were usually well received even though they related to small business and the ITI executives who were always in attendance took particular heed of my input as a small practitioner.

Once I had the unpleasant task of receiving from a West of Ireland client serious allegations about a senior ITI person. In a bit of a quandary I called on an ex-President of ITI that I knew and was advised that I had a duty to inform the current President right away.

When I did so the senior person resigned the very next working day citing family reasons.

While I felt that my action avoided considerable embarrassment for the ITI it appeared that they did not see it that way and relations between the ITI and myself deteriorated after this incident.

In 2009 I had further problems with the ITI. In June I had written an article for the Sunday Business Post on the light touch religious orders suffer on taxation. At the end of the article it referred to me as a member of the Council of the ITI. This reference to ITI was at the request of a previous ITI press spokesman who wanted to raise the ITI flag where possible in the Sunday Business Post.

Two days after publication I got a letter from the President, Jim Ryan, suggesting that the reference to my membership of the ITI Council gave the impression that my comments were in fact ITI policy. The matter was quietly resolved by my agreement not to refer to ITI in future articles.

Despite some differences with Jim I always found him to be fair and courteous and handled his presidency role well. Jim is a nephew of the famous Minister of Finance from the 1970s – Richie Ryan - who died in 2019.

By this stage I was well aware that ITI was not entirely happy with me. In 2012 I was interviewed on RTE Prime Time with opposite views to Revenue person. An ITI staff person said that a senior executive spent hours looking at it the next day to see if I had broken any rules!

Because I was an independent member of the ITI Council as distinct from being a representative of a large firm I was often in receipt of complaints about the ITI from a variety of sources. Usually I passed them on to the executive in the same way that a politician might pass complaints to the civil servants. To be fair the executive usually tried to remedy the problem identified by the complaint

While I cannot report on the content of ITI Council meetings, suffice to say that they were very useful. Experienced practitioners discussed new legislative proposals and administrative changes in an informal way.

Meetings tended to be lengthy and there was usually a high attendance. Percentage attendance rates were issued at the end of each year and I was always close to the top. Some Council members from very big firms would sometimes, due to work commitments, be unable to attend. It only happened to me once as I had a large corporate reorganisation down the country on the day of an important Council meeting. Decorum required one to advise the Institute that one could not attend due to circumstances.

On another occasion a Council meeting clashed with a meeting of the Council of ISME where I was also a member. I got the consent of the President of ITI to leave early. In effect, I was at half the ITI meeting and arrived late for the ISME meeting. The message here is "don't get involved in too many bodies".

Compared to country based Council members it was far easier for me to get to a meeting being just half an hour away on the DART. Usually for a country based member the whole day was gone with travel both ways and attendance at the meeting. There were no travel expenses paid as service was voluntary and regarded as an honour among one's peers.

The Institute had to host functions around the country and as a result I became familiar with the top hotels including Hayfield Manor Cork, Druids Glen and Powerscourt Ritz Carlton in Co. Wicklow the Galmont in Galway City and the Lyrath in Kilkenny to name but a few. The events in the hotels were tightly managed timewise with lectures and meetings and with little opportunity to party. An odd time one might hear rumours of late night carousing but generally the tax profession tends to be staid and conservative. However, I would not agree that they are dull as the media often suggests. There are several UK produced training manuals in video from where the chief actor is known for his portrayal of two roles – the taxman and the undertaker!

The only significant incident I can recall from a Joint Revenue/Institute Conference was that an old Revenue hand once made unflattering comments about the tax advisory profession. Within a few days the national newspapers had the story and made hay with it. These comments were very much the exception and indeed I believe what are called "Chatham Rules" applied to such meetings. In effect the comments were made off-the record and not a precedent. It was a very useful exercise for both Revenue and the Institute to discuss matters informally.

In 2008 I gave a farm tax nationwide lecture for the Institute speaking in Sligo, Galway, Limerick, Cork, Portlaoise and Dublin. It was essential to have a script as attendees want something to bring home. However, a script alone was not enough as speaking points on the margin of each page would make the talk more informal and often more interesting for attendees. A very useful source of material for the speaking points was the questions from the audience. I found that after five lectures by the time I got to the final lecture in Dublin I had sufficient new material to almost provide a second lecture.

In 2011 I gave the farm lecture again with a speaker from Teagasc which was a new development. As the motorway system had improved the roads so much, just a single lecture was held in west Dublin which drew in practitioners from all over the country. In recent times technology has meant that most of the audience are at their own desks and the days of physical attendance are gone for good. A lecture now might have 20 in Dublin and 200 remote attendees.

The Institute made a significant name for itself with the quality of the lectures. Early on they made a conscious effort to prevent people from speaking who were just trying to drum up business for a new practice that they had set up. Also, attendees at lectures were given feedback forms to complete which marked the quality of the lecture. While ITI might only get back a small proportion of the forms, the extent of the feedback allowed them to accurately determine if the attendees had got value for money.

The highpoint of the ITI calendar year is the annual dinner usually held in the Burlington Hotel as very few venues can feed 800 people at the same time. During the Celtic Tiger years I used to host a table of 12 people and nobody ever refused the invitations. I think the attraction was often the speech by a guest of honour who was usually the serving Minister of Finance. At the 2008 dinner I was at a table near Minister Brian Cowen and had an opportunity to speak to him. His knowledge of tax law and practise was very impressive for a busy politician.

During my 13 year sojourn as a Council member and Director of ITI a significant profile was developed in the media. Originally ITI was the poor relation to the Institute of Chartered Accountants. As a result of the recruitment of very experienced PR people and indeed the efforts of the executive generally the ITI became a go-to body for comment not only on tax issues but also on general economic affairs.

Meetings with senior Revenue officials were part of the normal duties of ITI Council members. The Revenue officials said that they also found them useful in order to hear first-hand on issues from sources other than their own staff. Issues they said were sometimes presented by ITI to them in a more objective context than coming from a briefing by their own staff.

The Revenue Board members were always very friendly to me and went out of their way to address any concerns that I had. This was despite the fact that ITI had not put me at the head table! The Board members, for their part, were always very knowledgeable on the issues of the day and it was very clear to ITI that Revenue people promoted to the Board had got there on merit.

After a Council Meeting in March 2011 a senior executive of the ITI told me that they were getting rid of me off Council in the next election. I raised it privately with a staff person that I was friendly with. She said word was that the Big Four would run sufficient candidates to defeat me in the election. I duly resigned from the Council in April 2011. The

President, Andrew Cullen of the Bank of Ireland, sent me a nice letter of thanks. Andrew was a close relative of the famous TCD Historian Louis Cullen who had taught me Economic History.

My absence from Council did not last long. In early 2012 I was approached by two Council members who said that I should stand again and that there would be no election. In some years the Council might have five vacancies but only five candidates and in that situation no election was held. The information I was given turned out to be accurate as there were just two vacancies and two candidates. I was declared elected much to the annoyance of some people, especially the person who told me a year earlier that they were getting rid of me!

2012 was quite an eventful year in the context of relations between ITI and myself. Revenue was investigating a tax scheme provided to a family many years before and one family member who was not happy with the information we gave him made a complaint to ITI.

We hired John Lynch of Whitney Moore, Solicitors to act for us in the matter. There was very extensive correspondence and in September 2013 the ITI Investigation Committee decided that I had no case to answer. However, in January 2014 the complainant appealed the ITI decision to their newly appointed Independent Adjudicator.

Further exchanges of correspondence occurred between Whitney Moore and ITI. A box of documents was furnished by ITI to me under the Data Protection Acts 1988 and 2003. Exchanges of strong correspondence continued right up to the actual disciplinary hearing on 2nd March 2015.

The hearing was short as my barrister pointed out to the Investigation Committee that my case was out of order on the grounds that when the complainant made the complaint there was no right of appeal to an independent adjudicator. It followed that the Independent Adjudicator had no right to be involved at all.

In the days after the hearing my legal team said they expected ITI to make me an apology and hopefully that would be the end of the saga. With no apology after six months and with plenty of opportunity as I was a serving member of the ITI Council I began a Circuit Court action for damages. It was listed to be heard on 26th April 2017. However, with other pressing commitments I settled the matter for a payment by ITI to me which is reflected in Note 17 of the Annual Accounts for year ended 31st March 2017 at the Companies Registration Office. There was no non-disclosure agreement.

Now, when I renew my professional indemnity insurance there is a question on the proposal form – "Were you ever before a Disciplinary Tribunal"? I have to say yes and then have to explain that it was the professional body that I was before who had to pay me substantial compensation. The insurers find the situation very comical and all the more so that I was a Director and Council member of the professional body. While they laugh about it I feel that the situation is not helpful for me seeking insurance. Ireland has become a very expensive place to get cover whether motor, employer or professional insurance.

It would be wrong to be critical of ITI for its disciplinary process. The people involved have to try to gauge the effect of their decisions with the need to serve the public good. A person aggrieved by an adverse decision might go to the High Court so to a great extent it's a balancing act. Unfortunately, unlike say solicitors, anybody can call themselves a tax advisor and if not an ITI member will not be subject to any regulation. Since my case ITI have made changes to the disciplinary process and it appears that current complaints are investigated by the Taxation Disciplinary Board of the UK Taxation Disciplinary Scheme.[19]

---

[19] Bye-Law No. 1 effective 28th June 2019 available on ITI website states that "In this Bye-Law the term Board means the Taxation Disciplinary Board established by the UK Taxation Disciplinary Scheme".

My general experience with ITI was good and very useful. When you work as a sole practitioner it is advantageous to have interaction with others engaged in the same work. Often I got more out of a meeting of the Tax Administration Committee than I got out of a tax lecture that I had to pay for in order to attend.

Chapter 9
– Self-Employment

When I commenced being self-employed in March 1992 an experienced practitioner advised me that annual fees of €50,000 were required in order to run an office, pay a secretary and make enough to live for the year. In the first year we did achieve that, thanks to my wife who was Secretary, Office Manager and Credit Controller.

The sources of my new clients were many:

1. Co. Wicklow, where I was from, produced a lot of work very quickly. Fortunately I was elected Chairman of the Local Development Group at the same time as I became self-employed. A lot of people came to me with their tax problems. One man had annual sales of €5m but had no accountant.

2. Binder Hamlyn clients contacted me when I commenced to wish me well as I had previously dealt with them for many years. A management consultant in Drogheda, Denis Moynihan, was instrumental in bringing me the tax affairs of a very large corporate group where Binder Hamlyn were the auditors.

3. A former partner in Binder Hamlyn, Tom Moore, who resigned shortly after I commenced in business gave me some of the tax affairs of a group of clients he had brought with him out of Binder Hamlyn.

Dermot Byrne outside his Dún Laoghaire Office where he worked from 1992 to 2019.

4. People that I had known in college gave me their tax affairs. Typically they included some prominent company directors and a nationally known artist.

5. The forestry sector people knew me from my involvement for many years in that business. By sheer coincidence the tax law brought the harvesting contractors into the C2 subcontract system from October 1992 and a large number of them asked me to act for them.

6. Finally, I had the clients primarily in the West of Ireland that Frank Brennan gave me. They were mainly accountancy firms with small clients. When the Celtic Tiger arrived these clients often developed quickly into large firms. In one town in 1992 I was advised that one could buy the whole town for IR£1m (€1.27m). Professional fees rose in conjunction with the rise in property values.

I realised very early on in self-employment that a second opinion is essential in most complex tax transactions. I was fortunate in being able to call on experts in each area of tax who offered immediate and constructive advice. They included Mel Ó Cuinneagáin on corporation tax, Dermot O'Brien and Gabrielle Dillon on VAT, Margaret Connolly on CAT/CGT and Frank Brennan on corporate reorganisation. Without their assistance one could not provide, on one's own, a comprehensive advisory service to the public at the level we operated.

As advisor, primarily to accountancy firms, they tended to pass to me queries which were difficult and where a wrong answer could lead to litigation. In all the years of practice involving complex schemes and arrangements we never had a claim for incorrect tax advice. One claim did arise for a breach of company law rules involving us and two other advisors. It was settled by our insurers independently of our involvement and oddly the following year our professional indemnity insurance fell to an all-time low!

In the early days of being self-employed we got a lot of work from a Dublin firm Brian Phelan & Co where the tax person was Jimmy O'Byrne (no relation). The Byrnes with an 'O' are said to be nearer the Chieftains of Ireland than those without an 'O'. They sent us an appeal case where it was held that a seven bedroom house with a restaurant was a hotel. This meant that reconstruction costs attracted hotel capital allowances at 15% per annum against all income for the proprietors.

A lot of tax appeals had a rural flavour. In one case involving travel expenses a turf harvesting machine operator on PAYE had to drive 40 miles to the bog each morning to do the work. Revenue said that home-to-work expenses were not allowed. At the Circuit Court the evidence was that the person went from his house to his employer's yard each morning to collect a barrel of diesel and then went to the bog. He could not leave fuel overnight at the bog or it would be stolen. The judge ruled that the person started work at the employer's yard and was entitled to their travel expenses to the bog.

Another appeal involved the write off by ACC of loan interest due by farmers for land bought in the 1980s. Revenue argued that one could not claim a deduction for what was ultimately not paid. The Circuit Court agreed with them and the clients were forced to submit revised accounts.

In another rural case a forest harvesting company claimed the 10% corporation tax rate on its profits. The basis for the claim was that the trees were owned by a sawmill and that the company's work was part of the manufacturing process. The Appeal Commissioners did not agree but the Roscommon Circuit Court did. Revenue appealed to the High Court and it upheld the Circuit Court decision.

We had some amusing experiences with the forest contractors who came into the tax system in 1992 as the C2 rules were extended to them. Under the C2 rules the Revenue advised the principal who was paying the contractor what rate of tax to deduct on making payments. If the contractor was not in the tax system then 35% tax was deducted by the principal and paid directly to Revenue.

About half the contractors we took on as clients had drawn the dole while working but as an explanation for their prior activities it was ideal i.e. they were not working. The other half were generally small farmers and had never drawn the dole. Generally Revenue adopted a reasonable attitude and got a large new group of potential taxpayers into the system without a witch-hunt.

One forest contractor client in the middle of the Celtic Tiger period got approval from a bank for a €250K hire purchase facility for 100% finance on a new machine. The suppliers in Finland insisted that he attend their factory to familiarise himself with the latest electronic systems. This worked out at over €2,500 in terms of flights and hotels but he did not have it. We applied for and got an additional facility from the bank to cover this extra cost. However, he got the machine, repaid all to the bank and made a success of his business. This was a 101% loan on the machine.

In 1993 an incentive amnesty was introduced allowing people to pay 15% of undisclosed income and gains. Many people came to us with funds held in banks in the Isle of Man and Jersey which should have been declared in Ireland. They were concerned about it coming to the notice of the Irish Revenue via a tipoff from a separated spouse or a disgruntled employee. On payment of the 15% tax, the matter was rectified. Some people actually declared a non-existent income in order to secure the perceived advantage of qualifying for the amnesty. In one case this turned out to be illusory as Revenue very quickly saw through the actions. In another case the departing wife wrote to Revenue with full details of the offshore accounts and how they were funded. When Revenue wrote to our client seeking an explanation we were able to show the amnesty certificate so that for 15% the funds were now legitimate.

A number of queries came in from accountants who had construction clients engaged in UK based projects using Irish resident companies. The Irish Revenue was applying Irish C2 rules to the contracts which we felt was very odd. We wrote to Revenue HQ and they agreed that the Irish C2 rules did not apply to Irish companies on UK sites. This ruling was published in Tax Fax 7/6/02 which is a Tax Institute weekly news-sheet.

Around this time we were involved in a number of Section 50 student accommodation developments. Prospective purchasers were looking for 90% plus construction cost elements in developments. The construction cost became a deduction for rental income so the higher the percentage the better. On a strict reading of the legislation we believed that only the cost of the land actually under a building need be disallowed rather than the cost of the whole site. This interpretation boosted percentages allowable to close to 98% in many developments. It was never challenged by Revenue.

Because we were dealing with a lot of firms of accountants across the country we were a barometer for new departures. We started to get queries on properties let to foreign workers. Interest charges on residential development had been disallowed to try to calm the property market. It did not do so and the buyers of property now sought deductions for rental income interest. We suggested giving the tenants breakfast so that it might be a trade and not a rental situation. The old concept of the boarding house made a return.

We were successful in applications to Revenue for 'radical innovation' where companies had developed new products and processes to allow tax-free dividends to be declared. As we had built up a lot of precedence and technical information on the subject we drafted our own unofficial guidelines and had them published in the Irish Tax Review. This was due to the failure by Revenue or the Department of Finance to publish guidelines, despite a ministerial undertaking in the Dáil that they would.

There was some reaction from the profession but the best one came two weeks later at an ITI/Revenue social function where a very senior Revenue official said that they were happy with our unofficial guidelines and had asked the Department of Finance if similar Revenue Guidelines could now be published.

Around this time a client was sent to prison for failing to make a tax return. He was nominally a client in that he was un-cooperative and only rang us an odd time. The sentence was one month in prison and a fine of €1,000 or both. The court sentenced him some months before with a choice. The local Gardaí called out to tell him that he would be going to prison next day if the fine was not paid. He just said he would be waiting for them to collect him next day. Apparently the Gardaí adopt this attitude because most people on hearing this will pay up on the fine.

The Gardaí called the next day and brought him to Mountjoy Prison. He had to hand over his possessions and was given a prison outfit. The Governor said that they had no room and he would be sent home the next day. He was put in with two Dubliners who were in on burglary charges. They fell around laughing when the client told them he was in for not making a tax return. The client formed the opinion that armed robbers were at the top of the prison hierarchy and he was at the bottom.

The next day he duly got his belongings back and a stamped card to say he had spent one night in prison and was discharged due to lack of space. He had his own money returned but he heard others being released say to the prison officer that they had no money to get home. They then got money to buy a bus ticket and a meal on the way home! To this day he has not paid the €1,000 fine and does not intend to pay it as he says one night in Mountjoy was worth €1,000 to him!

Being jailed in the UK for tax affairs was a very different matter. A former client, who was professionally qualified, moved to London after a construction crash here in the late 1980s. He apparently failed to file timely VAT returns in the UK and got two years in prison which he was required to serve. A custodial sentence for tax offences in the UK is very much more likely than here, especially if you were an Irish person living in the UK in the 1990s.

From about 2002 extraordinary prices were being paid for property. One sensed that all was not well when banks were offering 100% mortgages and an advance of 6% for stamp duty and legal fees. In the West of Ireland we had one case where land bought six years before for its agricultural value made nearly €5 million as it was close to a town and the owner had secured rezoning for residential development.

Around this time several clients acquired helicopters. They were useful if one was involved in business activities in different parts of the country and in the UK as many were. The most popular machine was the Robinson R44 which cost about US$250,000 at that time. Quite a few learned to fly their helicopter and got a licence which qualified them to fly on their own without any passengers. If one had to hire a pilot to fly the helicopter, it became very expensive to operate.

Several pilots whom I knew were not licenced to carry passengers invited me to fly with them but I always made an excuse and ducked out. I was aware from general chit-chat that navigation skills were not great and these pilots had a genuine fear of hitting powerlines which are hard to spot in the countryside. Apparently the trick was to see the line of pylons and that told the pilot there were lines there to avoid.

In the middle of the Celtic Tiger boom I had to attend a meeting involving clients where everybody present except myself had a helicopter. The subject I had to advise on was VAT issues on the purchase of a jet plane. For me this marked the peak of the Celtic Tiger period.

Business people with shops and farms trading well got into property development as they heard about spectacular profits. Later on came the professionals involved in the transactions such as solicitors and accountants. They saw their clients making quick profits and they thought they could do the same. Very often looking at their involvement in retrospect, it was too late. They tended to invest at the top of the market and as a result were always under pressure even before the crash came.

Many of our accountancy clients were very hard hit in the crash. Typically they were on the golf course with the local bank manager and had leveraged their property purchases with maximum debt and minimum equity. When the crash occurred the bank manager was transferred and the replacement was not a person who played golf. The new person just wanted the loans repaid which often proved impossible. Nobody could get finance even though a business owner might have very impressive accounts. One wondered why the reckless lending was allowed to continue for so long and only ceased when the banks could not borrow further on the international markets.

In 2005 we won two decisions at Appeal Commissioners which appeared to cast considerable doubt on the effectiveness of existing legislation.

The author, Joe Tiernan, had written a book on the Dublin Monaghan bombings of 1974. Revenue disputed his claim for artistic exemption. At the Hearing, Revenue had an expert from the Arts Council there but she did not offer any evidence to disagree with our expert, Professor Declan Kiberd, from the English Department of UCD. The Appeal Commissioner ruled in our favour due to the looseness of the guidelines. Based on that decision it appears that a lot of other books were then approved by Revenue for the relief.

The other significant appeal in 2005 was held in Tralee where Revenue was claiming that funds withdrawn from a close company via the sale of shares to a connected company were liable to Schedule F income tax under section 817. John O'Callaghan who was a very experienced

Appeal Commissioner ruled that section 817 was void for uncertainty and the Cape Brandy principle applied.[20] While Revenue said they were going to the High Court they never did. The decision gave a boost to cash extraction schemes which were on hold previously due to section 811 which is the general anti-avoidance rule.

Being a tax advisor allows one to have a unique insight into business. One sees the three generations of most businesses on the SME scale. The Founder drives the business hard, the next generation not so hard and the third generation sees it close down.

Very often now there is no succession, due to high education levels and people not being prepared to work all the hours required in a small or medium sized business. They can get well-paid secure employment with no risks associated with self-employment. Founders of businesses often seek to invest in property at a very early stage. Property is seen as a refuge from the uncertainty of trade. This created the classic trading structure in the Celtic Tiger days. A business consisted of a sole trader shop or garage. The trade was put into a company with the trader retaining ownership of the property which he let at a high rent to the company. The rental income from the company was not taxed as the property owner bought section 23 apartments to shelter the rent. The trading profits in the company were only taxed at 12.5%.

When the crash happened this structure was very hard hit. The property owner discovered that he did not have enough after-tax income to repay the capital on his borrowing. The solution was often to switch property let to a trading company into that trading company so the rent disappeared.

There is always snobbery in business with people with pubs and hotels being looked up to and those in say construction and haulage being looked down on. This tends to create a desire for operators at the perceived

---

20 *Cape Brandy Syndicate v IRC* [1923] 12 TC 358

lower end of the spectrum to try to acquire a pub or hotel. Nowadays, nobody would wish to buy a pub and the race has gone upmarket. This might explain why one very successful businessman tried to buy a bank but the timing was all wrong.

Many of my colleagues from 1974 in the Revenue training school became District Inspectors. This turned out to be very useful for me if I had a particular problem with a client in some part of the country. I did not abuse the connection and in return always found Revenue staff willing to help. Indeed some inspectors went out of their way to help me even though we had never met at all.

An interesting aspect of the appointment of some of my colleagues as District Inspector that they were then invited to join several local charitable organisations, typically the Knights of Columbanus, Rotary or the Lions Club. Generally they tended to avoid secret societies. One District Inspector said to me that if the Garret Fitzgerald-led government would not appoint Sean Patrick Bedford, who was the Supreme Knight of Columbanus, to the Board of Revenue, why would he join the Knights? He did join Rotary.

Many people were upset by the publication of names as tax defaulters. I found people very scared of being published. In one instance I was asked to advise on the tax audit of a lawyer who had already spent a large amount of money on the entertainment of key people in order to be made a District Court Judge. If on the defaulter list, the money was wasted. I made about 20 voluntary declarations much to the satisfaction of the tax auditor so there were no publications.

In another case, a farmer who it seemed was made liable for his father's tax liabilities had his settlement published the day before his land was used for the National Ploughing Competition. What unfortunate timing! Most publications are a nine-day wonder and people forget about them. However, in clubs, committees and bodies like a school board of management publication can be a cause for resignation from the position held.

I assisted Frank Brennan with his hotel developments. Typically he put together a structure whereby the investors could claim the construction cost of the hotel against their Irish rental income. I then helped him to find investors and in the Celtic Tiger period there were many. The official opening of the Lyrath Hotel in Kilkenny was an uncomfortable experience for me. At least three investors said they would attend via their own helicopters. On the day there was fog to ground level. When I heard a machine overhead I looked up anxiously in case there would be a collision. Fortunately only two turned up and there was a ten minute interval between them and neither of them landed due to the lack of visibility.

In the middle of the Celtic Tiger period the Government decided to put a cap on the tax shelter write-offs so that everybody would pay a certain amount in tax. The decision was based on a Revenue statistic that 242 people with income over €100,000 paid no income tax.

The implementation of the proposal was a very nasty shock to the people riding the Celtic Tiger and coincided with the crash. Many people suffered depression, marriage breakups and financial ruin in the ensuing years. One investment activity that I was involved in with forestry was often made 30 years before and suddenly at the clear-fell stage the profit above €80,000 was to be liable to income tax. After much lobbying we succeeded in getting forestry taken out of the restricted income list.

The annual conference of the Tax Institute was also a high point of the year in that the material was always of a high standard with at least one paper being outstanding. As it was held in a hotel there was always some alcohol consumed. People would tell me they were in the bar until 5 a.m. and I could never get past midnight!

One year I went to the conference with Frank Brennan in his car. The Dublin-Galway motorway was under construction so the old road was still in use. He was able to name many businesses on the way down saying who owned them and how they acquired them. It was a unique running commentary on the business activities in the towns through which we passed. On the return journey he gave me a litany of his recent unfortunate experiences.

Frank appeared before the Circuit Court Judge in a dispute with Revenue about Tax Reliefs. Revenue was represented by a Senior Counsel in a 3 piece pinstripe suit who introduced himself to the Judge. Frank then gave his name and said he was a Tax Consultant. The Judge exclaimed "Ah, the sports coat brigade". Frank protested that he was entitled to be there as an Associate of the Irish Tax Institute. The Judge then, with some reluctance, agreed.

A few weeks after that he had to attend a funeral in City Quay. He did not know the relatives of the deceased but shook hands with all of the chief mourners in the front seat of the church. As he was leaving he noticed a second funeral arriving and he enquired who that person was only to be told that it was the funeral he thought he was attending.

Finally, the previous week he represented a person at a tax appeal. The Revenue said they wanted the evidence under oath. Frank said his client had no problem with that. Frank turned to the client to indicate to him to go up to the witness box. The client shook his head and told Frank that as he was Jewish he would not swear on the Bible. Frank apologised to the Appeal Commissioner and explained the situation. It was then agreed that client could give evidence without the oath and the bible.

After this Frank asked me did I think there was a jinx on him. I disagreed and suggested that the incidents were the result of a busy professional life. By the time we got to Dublin he was treating the events as what they were, funny incidents as the late Paddy Crosbie used to say on his radio programmes long ago.

2008 saw the introduction of a new VAT on property system so that all the knowledge accumulated over many years was now redundant. The new system was designed to simplify the VAT system but in fact it made it more complex. Not only was there a new VAT system but there was a second new system for transitional property arrangements, especially leases, in existence with many years to run.

The VAT on property is a tax adviser's staple diet as the fees tend to be substantial with considerable risks should the advice be incorrect. A practise has grown up of accountants sending VAT on property queries to a third party even though they are often able to deal with it themselves. They are just subcontracting the risk to another firm.

Considerable claims and litigation have arisen even over such basic reliefs as the transfer of business relief. The Revenue has not helped the situation by sometimes changing their own position although there has been no change to the actual legislation. It is hoped that the present system will be allowed to settle in and that the rush for change sometimes manifests in official circles will not be entertained.

A good example of what I mean is that the replacement of the Appeal Commissioners system that stood for many years with a system that appears so far not fit for purpose. There is too much emphasis on procedures and too little on results.

The removal of the Circuit Court from the system was unfortunate. Over the years we always had three or four such cases a year. The judges brought fresh thinking to the tax law arguments and set the issues in a far wider legal context. Judge Olive Buttimer remains my favourite judge, as she was so competent, and we had many cases before her on the Southern Circuit. As far as I can recall we only lost two of which one was a test case to get a deduction for CGT for inheritance tax paid.[21] Her decisions were so good that they were generally not appealed to the High Court.

---

21 See reference to that court decision in Revenue Tax and Duty Manual 19-02-10 paragraph 10.14 and The Taxation of Capital Gains (FA 2018) page 169 published by Irish Tax Institute.

Given that we were involved in a lot of tax litigation and we had to hire counsel frequently. The late Tommy McCann and the late Paddy Hunt were of great assistance. More recently Edward Dwyer and Aoife Goodman provided very wise legal options and representation in court. Sometimes clients will select their own counsel where there is a lot at stake and the particular counsel had advised them in the past. In a tax case in the High Court the normal position is that there is a senior and junior counsel and a solicitor (who is instructing them) must also be present. We lost one particular High Court action where we were financing the case ourselves. Costs were duly awarded against us. When we appealed the decision to the Supreme Court, Revenue said that they would pay their own costs if we dropped our appeal which we promptly did.

In recent years the newspapers have reported extensively on what is variously called the Value Shift Scheme or the Share Rights Transfer Scheme. It has also turned up in several Dáil questions. It had its origins in some research undertaken by Frank Brennan and myself many years ago. I will describe how it operates as readers will often have heard of tax schemes but few will understand how they operate.

Suppose you own a trading company, OldCo Ltd, with a base cost of €2 and it has now ceased trading and there is €2m in its bank account. In order to get the funds out of the Company into personal ownership the shareholders will suffer capital gains tax at 33% or €666,000 approximately.

With the Value Shift Scheme the shareholder incorporates NewCo Ltd and subscribes for 1,000 ordinary shares in it for €1,000. The other company OldCo Ltd then subscribes for 1,000 B ordinary shares in NewCo Ltd at a premium of €1,999 per B ordinary share. This means that OldCo Ltd has invested €1,000 for the par value of the B ordinary shares and €1,999,000 for the share premium or a total of €2m.

At a meeting of NewCo Ltd sometime later the rights to the ordinary shares and the B ordinary shares are swapped. This means that the individual who subscribed €1,000 for the ordinary shares now has access to the share premium account on the B ordinary shares. As all the parties are related or are connected the base cost of the 1,000 ordinary shares now has become €2m.

The following day NewCo Ltd is put into liquidation and the individual gets €2m out of the Company free of Capital Gains Tax as a connected party. OldCo Ltd subscribed €2m for the shares and thus there is no gain.

Of course Revenue does not accept that the scheme works as described and the issue is now before the courts. Central to the Revenue argument is that the swap of rights to shares in a dividend for the individual shareholder. As of November 2020, a test case held is under appeal to the Court of Appeal which is the level immediately below the Supreme Court.

Chapter 10 – Conclusion

The nature of Tax Advisory work has radically changed over the last 45 years. Apart from knowing the tax rules one now has to be computer savvy in order to interact with Revenue. As the electronic system has expanded the old paper system has shrunk.

The Revenue Online System (ROS) allows the immediate calculation of liabilities as soon as a Return is complete. This facilitates the early and correct payment of taxes due. The common problem in a professional office of the loss of documents is no longer a problem if they are in the electronic system and can be recalled when needed.

The disadvantages with the electronic system are an over dependence on technology and access to it by unauthorised persons with malicious intent. Taxpayers do not like giving Revenue access to their Bank Accounts in order to take Direct Debits from their Accounts to pay taxes. Fraudsters have circulated false Revenue documents complete with the Harp seeking confidential banking information. It is sometimes very difficult even for practitioners to decide what is false and what is genuine. I have even come across an experienced business person taken in by the Nigerian "10m Dollars in a trunk" story seeking one's bank details to get the money out of that country.

Tax work falls into two parts – compliance and consultancy. Compliance means completing and submitting Tax Returns which are now subject to tight time limits. If not met then a surcharge will arise on Income Tax

Returns and for other types of Claims for Tax Relief the claim may be too late so that no tax refund arises. If a practitioner has the records to do the work he has really no excuse for being late with the work. It is useful to advise clients when seeking their annual records that if they are received within 2 months of the date for the relevant tax payment then the practitioner will not be liable for any late filing consequences. Increasingly there is a tendency to charge extra fees for last minute suppliers of records. This can often be the most effective way to deal with them.

Tax consultancy work is less time constrained than compliance work. Often one is asked to advise on how to arrange a transaction that involves the least tax charge for a client. Typically one will have plenty of time to prepare a response and if the advice is ultimately disputed by Revenue it may be quite a long time before this is recognised. However, the consequences may be far more severe than an error in compliance work. Also, as a long time may have elapsed since the work was done then the key people involved may no longer be available to consult. A practitioner must retain good records here not just for 4 years but for such time as it is reasonable to conclude that Revenue is not going to challenge the arrangements.

A business guru has described an entrepreneur as a person who can live with uncertainty. Such a quality is a very useful attribute for a tax advisor. There are always a number of issues with clients and with Revenue. One can get bad news one day and good news the next day. It is necessary to be optimistic and see the bright side of matters so that one can take adversity in one's stride. In the Letter of Engagement with your client do not promise results that cannot be achieved. The other advantage of a Letter of Engagement is that one has also an agreed amount due for the work once it is complete.

Why should one decide on a Tax Advisory career? Most of the people I have worked with said that they sort of fell into it by accident. It is not like deciding in school that one would like to be a teacher or a nurse or whatever. For myself an interest in current affairs was instrumental in taking me towards tax work. I recall as a student listening to the Budget Speech of Richie Ryan in May 1973 while attending TCD Sports Day. The porter told me to turn off the radio or he would confiscate it as a guest of honour President DeValera could not hear what the Provost was saying! In the 1930s DeValera was always very friendly towards the College despite its British tradition and in return over the years he was often the guest of honour in Trinity Week.

As a tax advisor you will be asked to attend important company meetings as tax has become crucial in transactions. In the old days the Auditor might attend such meetings but few would wish to talk to him or her even though they have specialist knowledge. It is just that tax is more important. A tax advisor should approach a meeting of the directors of a Company with the brief that the proposals must stand up commercially first and if they do then try to make them tax efficient. People often want to do things the other ways round i.e. tax first and commerciality last.

Very few tax advisors have all round skills. Some may be technically very competent but poor on after sales service. Others may lack the personality and contacts to develop the practice and get in new business. The failing I was always most conscious of was my failure to remember faces and names. I have lost some clients by not being able to identify them and they then assumed I had snubbed them. It is also very trying to chat to somebody who clearly knows who you are but you do not recognise them. It hits me most afterwards – once I was sitting next to a Tax Appeal Commissioner but only realised afterwards who it was! How not to conduct oneself as a Tax Practitioner!!

Marketing was always my strong point. From the day I commenced self-employment the work came in at a steady pace. Some of my colleagues were of the opinion that I should join a large practice with a brief to just get in business. However, that never appealed to me as being one's own boss was something I really appreciated.

In the 2004/2009 Boom I had to turn away a lot of business due to pressure of work. In the subsequent Crash many of these prospective clients did not survive so perhaps my loss of opportunity was not significant. My general strategy was to look after the client who paid promptly. This is always a sound approach to business.

This book is intended for the people who work within the Irish Tax System be it in the Professional side or the Revenue side of the system. This book hopefully fills a gap in the now extensive Irish Tax literature. If the reader needs a tax advisor or has any comment on the book you can access me at my email address info@dermotbyrnetax.ie.

Dermot Byrne, Dublin. December 2020.